What if GOD Asks YOU to DO Something…

Weird?

Finding God's Path

Jan Hibma Hofstra

Jan Hibma Hofstra (signature)

What If God Asks You To Do Something Weird?
Finding God's Path

For information:
Janice Hofstra
janhofstra8@gmail.com

Scripture quotations are from the NEW KING JAMES VERSION of the Bible. Copyright 1979,1980,1982, Thomas Nelson Inc., Publishers.

Scripture quotations taken from the HOLY BIBLE NEW INTERNATIONAL VERSION, Copyright 1973, 1978, 1984 by International Bible Society.

Scripture taken from THE AMPLIFIED BIBLE, Old Testament copyright 1965, 1987 by the Zondervan Corporation. The Amplified New Testament copyright 1958, 1987 by The Lockman Foundation. Used by permission.

Scripture quotations marked KJV are from the KING JAMES VERSION of the Bible.

Cover Design by Jan Hibma Hofstra

Cover Image by Daniel K. Williams

Photographs by Charity Swindell

Published in the United States of America
Hofstra, Jan Hibma
What if God Asks You To Do Something Weird?
Finding God's Path/Jan Hibma Hofstra

DEDICATION

This book is dedicated to my mother, Betty Hibma, who encouraged me to go on my mission trip to Haiti and was one my biggest supporters in writing this book. She has a huge giving heart and is the one who first taught me how to love and to care about others.

I also dedicate this book to my grandchildren, who I pray will walk with God and do supernatural exploits for His glory. And, that they will know that living for Jesus is the most important thing you can ever do in this life.

Contents

Preface

1	Unexpected Surprises	3
2	Who Goes There?	14
3	Even In The Darkness	23
4	The Seed	34
5	Trouble On The Pathway	49
6	The Pit of Fear	58
7	If You Make Your Bed In Hell	69
8	Hopelessness	83
9	A Plan For Me	99
10	The Orphanage	123
11	Connections	148
12	Provision	157
13	Divine Appointments	168
14	Rerouting A Hurricane	189
15	Epilogue: Making A Difference	195

PREFACE

Dear Reader,

Has God ever asked you to do something uncomfortable? You know the moment; suddenly, you know what God wants you to do, but, even the thought of it, ties your stomach up in knots. It could be something as simple as meeting the new neighbor next door with a plate of cookies, or paying for groceries for the person in front of you in line at the store because they were short money. It might be something big and complicated, like going on a mission trip to a foreign country or teaching a Sunday School Class.

"Me, God? God, I just couldn't!" You balk and squirm, but you know you need to step out, and obey the Holy Spirit's voice. Even Moses stood in those shoes, and he told God, "Can't you find someone else to do the job?" I have felt the same way sometimes too, haven't you?

But God planned for us to touch others lives by living His plan and not our own. Journey with me to Haiti after the massive earthquake in 2010. Meet some of the people, walk the dusty streets and then, in the quietness of your everyday life, hear the whispers of God's plans for your own life. Come with me and explore how you can live a remarkable life, filled with divine appointments, answered prayer and overflowing provision. Then, step into the destiny that God has prepared, especially for you!

I hope you will join me, as we discover God's planned adventures!

Jan Hibma Hofstra

MY DEEPEST APPRECIATION TO:

My husband, Peter Hofstra, my daughter, Sarah Wright, and my mother, Betty Hibma, Carl Hibma, Beth & Daniel Williams, Michelle Dudley, Dr. Nancy Johnson, George & Florence Altidor, Paul Morrow Jr., Chuck & Charity Swindell, Macrae & Ariel Saunders, Michelle & Randy McKisick, Rodney Wehrenberg, Pastor John & Kathy Arthur, and all of my mission team members, as well as Pastor Tommy Barnett and Pastor Don Landers.

Chapter 1

U NEXPECTED SURPRISES

What can you expect when you do anything for God? Expect the unexpected! When you have lined up your ducks in a row, and then poof, they are suddenly scattered, you know you are in for a God adventure!

Make a decision as you embark on this journey called life, to set your heart like the helm of a great ship, ready to follow the course of the Lord no matter where it leads. Be determined to not get upset over changes that didn't go according to *your* plans, and then you will behold God's design unfolding before you, supernaturally.

"We are making our final descent into to Port-au-Prince," the pilot said in a low voice. The intercom clicked off. I peered out the small window of the plane trying to see what this new strange country looked like. The plane was making its way over the mountains in Haiti. The sun was going down and washing a golden haze over everything in its sight as it said its last good-bye.

"How are we going to get through the airport before darkness falls?" I thought. When darkness begins in Haiti, its curtain falls abruptly.

Darkness can be a dangerous time around the airport in Port-au-Prince. The US State Department has even imposed a curfew for their embassy employees when night falls in downtown.

Our plane was now over two hours late to arrive, and I resolved myself to the fact that maybe no one would be meeting us at the airport to help us through customs.

I leaned back in my seat, and the fasten seat belt sign above lit up, accompanied by the announcement that we must now stay in our seats.

Daydreaming, my mind drifted back to the night before. I was in an ice cream parlor, licking a chocolate ice cream cone, sitting next to my husband, Peter and across from George and Florence, a wonderful Haitian couple that we had met two weeks earlier.

"Janice, would you like to have my cousin...help your group through customs like they do for the diplomats?"

We were sitting in a booth discussing Haiti and Jesus. George and Florence were telling us about the people of Haiti and the culture from a native Haitian's point of view. Time flew past, and a couple of hours seemed like a few minutes. Peter checked his watch in surprise. "I guess we need to call it a night since we have to get up early to leave for Haiti tomorrow morning," he said.

Florence flashed a wide smile and leaned in, "Janice, would you like to have my cousin Juan meet you at the airport and help your group get through customs like they do for the diplomats? He works for one of the embassies in Port-au-Prince. It would make the process so much easier! I am sure that my cousin would love to help!" she said enthusiastically. Then her face changed and her eyes flashed as she changed her tone, "The airport in Haiti can be a nightmare! In Haiti, it takes a long time to get through customs as they go through all your things, and

> *"The airport in Haiti can be a nightmare..."*

you have to wait in a long line to get your passport stamped. In the parking lot, you have to watch out for people that will try and steal your bags or try to carry them to extort money from you. They can be very persistent," she said with fire in her soft brown eyes. "Juan will make it smooth for you," she offered, "It is God's favor!"

The plane was descending even lower now, and I was jolted back to the present. The little specks on the mountains were now becoming trees, as the ground drew closer into view. "Here we are!" I thought. What an eventful day this had been already. Starting early, we rose out of bed easily, full of excitement for the long awaited trip. "Today's the day!" I said to Peter, as I turned back the covers and jumped out of bed. We were already packed, so getting ready by six in the morning was easy.

Making one last check to make sure I had my malaria medicine before Sarah, our daughter, picked us up to take us to the airport, I slid back the zipper on the pocket of my carry-on, and it came off in my hand. " What in the world? I just bought this bag!" I decided I could shift the contents into another pocket. Pulling back a second zipper, the unthinkable happened; it too came off in my hand. "What is going on here?" I was now beginning to panic. In five minutes, we were supposed to be leaving for the airport, and now, I have a broken carry-on.

> *Pulling back a second zipper,… it too came off in my hand…. I was now beginning to panic.*

"Peter!" I yelled, "I just broke my carry-on!"

Peter came through the living room to survey the situation, "I know where your old green bag is in the attic," he offered. In a minute he was back with my faithful old bag that I had set aside because of the wear on it. I repacked quickly and finished just in time to hear the doorbell ring.

Travel Delays and More!

We got to the airport right on time. Our group made it through security enduring the whirling glass machines that virtually undressed you and then spit you out, only then to be patted down. We sat in the lobby area drinking last minute coffee and finally boarded the plane right on schedule.

Our plane from Tulsa pulled onto the runway to take off, and then it stopped. We just sat there as the air in the plane became stuffy.

Our plane from Tulsa pulled onto the runway to takeoff and then... stopped.

The excitement of our trip began to melt like ice cubes in warm tea, as the reality of a travel delay settled over us. We sat for an hour on the airplane, while they fixed an electrical problem. Because of the delay, we got to Miami late. We had planned to have exotic Cuban food in the airport and take a leisurely bathroom break before boarding our next flight, but all of our plans dissolved in the long corridors of the airport, as we ran to catch the connecting flight.

Ten of us made it to the connecting gate, our hearts pounding and out of breath. The other four people on our team had gotten stuck in the back of the first airplane. "You better hustle onto the plane before they leave you," the stewardess in the crisp blue uniform said. Paul, our mission's coordinator, told her that the rest of our group was just behind us.

> "Can't you wait for them?" he pleaded.

"Can't you wait for them?" he pleaded.

"Sorry Sir. There is nothing I can do. We are closing the doors behind you. Hurry on." Still gasping for breath, we hustled down a skinny ramp that led to our airplane and then up the airplane stairs. They shut the door behind us with finality. Four of our team members would miss the flight; Pastor John, Charity, Chuck and Rodney. They would not let them on the plane even though it was still sitting at the gate. With no time to load them, surely our bags would miss the flight too.

"Pastor John has our contact information," I whispered to Peter, "How will we know who to call when we get there?" I assumed that we were supposed to call when we arrived for our ride to the base camp.

"Let's pray," Peter whispered back. Silently, we began to pray. The plane backed out and gave the usual announcements. It sat for five minutes, then ten, then fifteen minutes.

Then the intercom clicked back on, "We have a problem with a pressure valve. We will need to go to another gate for maintenance." The gate number we were going to was a long way from where the plane was presently sitting.

> *Then the intercom clicked back on, "We have a problem with the pressure valve..."*

"Can our team members get on the plane now?" I asked the stewardess in the aisle.

"No," she said flatly, "We have closed the flight." Peter stood and then disappeared down the narrow plane aisle. When he came back, he told me what had happened.

"I went to the front of the plane and asked the head stewardess if our other members could get on the plane," he smiled with a twinkle in his eyes. "She turned to the captain who still had his door open and had overheard everything."

Peter imitated the pilot's voice with a southern drawl, "If they can make it, I don't see why not." I giggled at his impersonation. "I called Pastor John and told him our gate number. They are headed our way," he beamed.

Oddly, the whole plane of strangers cheered and clapped as they came down the aisle.

In a few minutes, all four of our missing team members appeared. Oddly, the whole plane of strangers cheered and clapped as they came down the aisle. The plane was full of missionaries who had overheard us communicating about the problem across our many different seat assignments.

"It was God who broke the plane!" a cheery looking woman across the aisle wearing a bright yellow dress that was as loud as her voice proclaimed boisterously, and the whole plane seemed genuinely happy about it. It was as if God was saying to us, "Look, I have miracles in store for you, my hand is upon you! This is my trip, my plan. Trust in me, and let me show you my glory."

Chapter One: Unexpected Surprises
Study It!

1. In chapter one, what surprise events happened to Jan that she needed to be flexible?

2. Why do you think God wants us to be flexible, whether we are on a mission trip, or just the mission of every day life?

3. What events in your own life have surprised you? Why?

4. Are you currently facing a situation that you need to let God have control and release your grip? If so, what is it?

5. Read Philippians 4:6. What are your requests today? What prayer can you pray to thank God that He is working on your behalf in these specific situations? Write it out.

Chapter 2

Who Goes There?

What kind of people step out to do exploits for God? Maybe you think you are not "that type of person" or it just isn't "your thing." That is what I thought. Going to a third world country wasn't on my radar. I don't like dirty places. I have a strong sense of smell, and bad smells turn my stomach. My bus tour to Italy flashed through my mind confirming it. On this pleasure trip, I remembered having to use gross, stinky bathrooms with no toilet seats. Horrified one day, I discovered only a hole in the floor in place of the toilet and with no door! "I can't use that thing!" I proclaimed to the waiting line.

You might feel like I did or maybe not, but only through dependence on God, by giving Him permission to send you wherever He wants to send you, will you ever make an eternal impact. Don't just assume what God's plans are, because you don't want to do something. Pray about opportunities, then listen for His answers. Who goes there? Anyone! Maybe, even you!

Our mission team was an interesting lot, including the young and the older.

There were people you would expect, like the two pastors and people you wouldn't dream of going, like me.

One of the pastors was John, the preacher of our church. He is full of love and compassion for others. Last year he went to Mexico, even after everyone else cancelled because they thought the trip was too dangerous. Pastor John loves missions and is undaunted by danger.

Another pastor on the trip was Pastor Teodulo. He is the preacher of the Mexican church that meets in our building on Thursday nights. He is an elegant, physically fit, Mexican man in his early forties with a kind face who speaks only a small amount of English, but understands a lot of it. On the way home he ate a salad in the airport, while the rest of the group ordered cheese burgers. His accomplice was Elder, a member of his church. As Pastor Teogulo was thin, Elder was round.

Elder's keen sense of humor made the trip a lot more pleasant. He told me a funny story in the airport that had me laughing uncontrollably. "Sometimes I have had problems communicating in Spanish," he confessed. "I am from Guatemala, not Mexico.

When I first came to America, I was at a church potluck and was telling them how much I loved a type of Guatemalan bread. Everyone got really quiet," he said. "They looked at my wife and me strangely. Then the pastor confessed to me that I had just told them in Spanish that I loved prostitutes. You should have seen my wife blush!" he chuckled.

"The pastor confessed to me that I had just told them in Spanish that I loved prostitutes. You should have seen my wife blush!" he chuckled.

Paul, the mission trip coordinator works on airplanes for a living. His boyish face and trim figure disguise the fact that he is really in his fifties, but the down to earth wisdom he shares let you know he is no green horn to missions.

He brought with him an outspoken 21 year old named Frank. This was his first mission trip. Tall and lanky, Frank's personality is as bold as the color of his bright red hair.

In a good recipe, every ingredient is important, just like Rodney was to our mix. He added strength and joy to the team by his disposition. He would do anything that was asked of him, always with a smile.

Charity was an unlikely pick for the trip, that is what I thought at first. Before the trip Charity and I discussed going to Haiti in her office one day, "I am nervous about going to Haiti!" she confessed to me. "Chuck wants me to go, but I am not so sure about the trip!" I knew how she felt. At least she had the boldness to sign up to go right away.

She became our team's unofficial photographer and magically captured photos of many, many moments on our journey. Her importance to our trip was invaluable. After we got home, she made a power point presentation of the trip set to music. It made a huge impact on our whole congregation, giving them a taste of what it was like to be in Haiti. Of course, God knew what he was doing when he chose Charity for this trip.

Her husband, Chuck, is excited about missions; he had been on many trips before and knew it would be life changing.

Randy, Charity's dad was on the trip too. Quiet, warm and easy to talk with, he made the trip fun.

"Two hundred people showed up to fill the job,...they hired only four and I was one of them."

Michelle, his wife, is a tender hearted beauty. She has trouble hiding the tears that fill her big blue eyes when she sees people in heart breaking conditions. She became my prayer partner and was an important part of the trip for me.

The two youngest people on the trip were only teenagers, but these girls were excited about missions. Ariel got a job as a waitress to get money to go on the trip. "Two hundred people showed up to fill the job," she confided, "They hired only four, and I was one of them!" Macrae got a job too and saved her money, eager for the experience.

Peter, my husband, was part of the team, a man of great faith; I will get to his story later. Tall and husky with magnificent green eyes and salt and pepper hair, insightful and outspoken; he has a compassion that sees people that others find invisible, looking past the exterior to their needs and always reaching out to help them.

And me, the most unlikely candidate! I cut my long blonde hair to just below my shoulders to go on the trip, hoping it would help me "blend in" to minister better in Haiti. When I told my sister Michelle, she laughed at me, "Janice, it doesn't matter that you cut your blonde hair. Your white skin will still make you stick out!" Of course, she was right!

Chapter Two: Who Goes There?
Study It!

1. Do you feel like God has specific plans for your life? Why, or why not?

2. Read Psalms 139:16 (NLT). "You saw me before I was born. Every day of my life was recorded in your book. Every moment was laid out before a single day had passed." What conclusions can you draw from this verse?

3. Describe how you would feel if you were asked to go on a mission trip to Haiti.

4. At times, people categorize themselves as a certain type of person. Analyze your life. Do you think that you are open to do whatever God calls you to do, even if it just isn't "you"? Explain.

Chapter 3

E VEN IN THE DARKNESS...

Expect God to answer your prayers, plain and simple. Do you ever pray and secretly think that nothing will happen? When you are out doing God's work, expect it to be *God's work*. Trust Him to accomplish great things for you and through you, in all situations, even in the darkness.

Finally, the moment had arrived. The plane touched down bumping down the runway and skidding to a stop.

At last we began the process of disembarking. It was 5:00 pm, and we were officially two hours late. Stepping off the plane, we gazed down a long expanse of pale green stairs. It was the first step to get through customs.

With all my heart I hoped to see the face of Juan, Florence's cousin. If Juan had waited for our late plane for two hours with the impending darkness, it would be a miracle. I had no idea what he looked like, but he was supposed to be holding up a sign. I remembered other trips where I walked past people holding up signs with names on them. I always wondered who they were meeting. Now it was my turn. I strained to see who was standing at the bottom of the stairs.

A Haitian man stood holding up a small sign, and I could see the name of our church on it. He was dressed in a crisp long sleeved white dress shirt and black dress pants, but his face is what I was drawn to because he had the same big brown eyes as Florence. "Juan!" Peter and I yelled in unison.

When we got to the bottom of the stairs Juan greeted us warmly, "Welcome to Haiti", he said shaking my hand, and then Peter's hand profusely. Next, he escorted us off to the side and gave each person in our group a custom form with a small yellow pencil. "Fill these out and I will be back," he said smiling. The other people from the plane filed past us, staring.

"Where did you get the forms?"they questioned..we raced to fill them out.

"Where did you get the forms?" they questioned. Ignoring them, we raced to fill out the forms on a long skinny table with no chairs.

"What are you supposed to put on question number three? What about question seven?" We put our heads together to decipher the meaning of the list of questions. So many questions! Soon, Juan returned and collected our cards. A bus arrived, and skidded to a stop. Suddenly the glass doors flew open and a blast of air escaped with a swoosh.

"Board this bus, and I will meet your group around the corner" Juan said. We obeyed. The bus took us around the side of the building, past a few warehouses like tin buildings. A huge rat about the size of a small cat came out of a pile of trash and scurried past the bus.

"Did you see that gigantic rat?" Rodney exclaimed.

"Eww!" I shivered. I hoped we wouldn't see any more. We rounded a corner and the bus came to a halt. Again, the door slid open, and we stepped out to see Juan waiting there. He ushered us right past customs where they were opening everyone else's bags. There was a long line of people waiting to be searched and others in the process of the inspection with their bags sprawled open, exposing all of their contents to the security personnel.

"Did you see that gigantic rat?" Rodney exclaimed.

"We walked right past them!" Peter whispered to me in amazement. I smiled back at him. "I know, don't you feel like royalty?" Elated, I glanced back at the line of tired people and felt a twinge of guilt.

This part of the airport terminal was a large tin building. It seemed like there were only a few dim, bare bulbs to light the whole building. It reminded me of one of those dark warehouses in the movies where the Mafia brings people to interrogate them. As dark as it was, it was also very crowded.

> *It reminded me of one of those dark warehouses in the movies where the Mafia brings people to interrogate them.*

In the stale thick air and the stifling heat, Juan directed us to get our bags. He pointed across the building, towards a huge pile of bags. Taking our passports he disappeared somewhere behind us. We fought through the mountain of bags in the faint light. We had cleverly decided to tag our bags with bright orange surveyor's tape; the only problem was another group had the same good idea. "Now whose bag is this?" One by one, after a little searching, we found them all. God had answered our prayer!

Juan came back with his hands full of all the

stamped passports. He smiled at me and then asked if we needed anymore help. "I don't think so," I stammered, "but thank you so very much! I will tell Florence hello!" I said, hoping that he could feel the appreciation in my voice. And with that, our knight-in- shining armor, disappeared into the shadowy terminal. I passed the passports in my hand back to each owner. Then, bags in tow, our group made our way to the outside.

A sickening smell blasted us, as the automatic doors swished open for us to leave the airport. The smell hung heavy in the air, wrapping its thick fingers around everything in sight, catching my breath away with its strange fumes of sulfur and trash and thronging humanity. I have never experienced this putrid smell before! "What exactly is it?" I wondered.

Another Answered Prayer

As quickly as the door had opened, there was suddenly mass confusion. A loud crowd of people were descending upon our small band like swooping vultures. The writhing throng was pushing and shoving and jostling for position, asking if they could carry bags, begging for money, a loud crowd of voices echoing in the darkness. A thin young white man held up a small sign with something scrawled on it, but in the confusion and pervasive darkness half of our team members walked right past him. Peter saw the name of our church on the sign and called for us to come back.

The thin white man had us follow a guide, but in the darkness, I wasn't sure who it was. "Don't let the man in black have your bags," Michelle whispered to me. There was a huge white guy dressed all in black with piercing blue eyes trying to help people with their bags. I began to pray.

"Don't let the man in black have your bags," Michelle whispered to me.

My bags were heavy, almost more than I could maneuver. We were taking supplies to the people of Haiti, as well as our clothes. The bottom suitcase was a smaller case packed to the hilt with every seam groaning, and the top was a big long duffle bag stuffed with things too. The load combined felt unbalanced and wobbly. I also had my large carry-on slung over my shoulder.

"Dear Jesus, Give me strength to pull this unsteady load and not to have it turn over. And God, please don't allow anyone to bother me or to ask to help me with my bags," I prayed silently.

I knew if someone grabbed them, the load would have toppled right over. I could picture in my mind's eye, five dark figures grabbing from every direction, making off with my bags. Time turned to slow motion; it felt like an eternity, pulling those bags across the uneven cobble stone side walk full of large pot holes, then across a really rough parking lot surrounded by a following horde. We were racing the darkness, trying to beat it, before it completely captured us with a curtain of inky blackness.

It took all of my strength to pull the huge load of heavy bags, and I was slowly lagging behind the group. Peter looked back at me with eyes full of sympathy, unable to help. To my relief we finally reached our destination, which was a tap tap parked at the far end of the lot. Our group piled into the back of it. I had never seen a tap tap before, but I had heard some hair raising stories about them from my father-in- law, who had been to Haiti many times.

A tap tap is like a pickup truck with the bed of the truck shrouded in a metal cage; inside the bed, there are long wooden benches on each side for the occupants to sit on. The outside of the truck is usually painted with bright colors that sometimes have religious sayings on them. In Haiti, tap taps are usually very crowded, often passengers are crammed in like sardines, sometimes with pigs or chickens in tow. At times, people ride on top of the roof, and it is common to see them hanging out the back of the truck as well. When Haitian people want to get off the tap tap, they tap on the roof or the windshield, thus the name tap tap. This particular tap tap was reserved just for our group so we did not have the massive crowding.

Many of the people on the team told of how hard it was to hold onto their suitcases because of the people trying to grab them.

I was relieved to finally be sitting inside. While we waited for Craig to get our bags situated in the other vehicle, we talked. Many of the people on the team told of how hard it was to hang onto their suitcases because of the people trying to grab them. A few Haitian men stood at the back of our tap tap asking for money.

"Please, you can give me some money, can't you?" We tried to ignore them, but it felt awkward. We were told not to give them any money under any circumstances, lest a crowd of others wanting money too, would develop and mob us. God had again miraculously answered my prayer. No one had tried to grab my bags or even ask to take my bags; they had not turned over on the uneven ground full of pot holes either.

The tall white guy who was trying to help people with their bags was Craig, the person in charge of picking us up and taking care of us.

Chapter Three: Even In The Darkness
Study It!

1. Hebrews 11:6, says that faith pleases God. Has God ever answered your prayers in an unexpected way? Explain.

2. Read Zec.4:6. How can this verse help you as you do God's work?

3. In chapter one, Florence says, "The airport in Haiti can be a nightmare!" After reading about it, what would be your biggest concern? Why?

4. Even in the darkness, God is working in your life. What darkness do you face in which you need a shaft of God's bright light?

Chapter 4

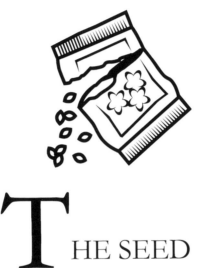

T HE SEED

Make no mistake about it, when you follow the Lord, sometimes you will get out of your comfort zone! If God asks you to do something that is uncomfortable and kind of strange, don't miss it by turning Him down. God will provide the comfort that you need, in the zone that He sends you. He has exactly what you need, whatever the assignment. Of course, God will never ask you to do anything that is against the Bible, His Holy Word, but He may ask you to live like you literally stepped into its pages.

Have you ever wondered at what point God begins to orchestrate events in your life to get you headed in the right direction? How far back in time does he have to go to get you to make a "right decision"?

This trip started long before I was aware of it. It started as a small seed planted by a Bible study I was a part of. We were studying 1 Chronicles 10:4 about a guy named Jabez.

Jabez seemed like just another guy in history, except for his terrible name, which meant pain because his mother gave birth to in him in pain. But, when I read the prayer that he prayed, the words jumped off the page and something in my heart caught on fire.

> *"Oh, that You would bless me indeed, and enlarge my territory, that Your hand would be with me, and that You would keep me from evil, that I may not cause pain".*
>
> *-1 Chronicles 4:10 (NKJV)*

The Bible tells us that God granted his request. The challenge the Bible study put forth was simple, "Will you pray this prayer too? Will you also cry out to God like Jabez did?" I was ready! I pondered the prayer, I bought a song of the prayer, I taught the middle school kids at church the prayer, and I, too, prayed the prayer. It burned in my heart! You never know the adventure that God will take you on when you give Him permission to expand your horizons beyond what you can see!

> "Will you pray this prayer too? Will you also cry out to God like Jabez did?"

Where will I go when I ask God to expand my territory? Could this prayer change my life too? That is where my journey begins. God began to put together little events in my life, like patches in a colorful quilt. Events, I didn't know would go together to complete His plan, until they were accomplished.

In the summertime, I renewed my passport because Peter suggested we take my mom to the Caribbean for a vacation. Little did I know, I would use it instead for a mission trip to a place I would never pick out of a glossy travel brochure!

And the next event was an event so awful I wouldn't think that God could use it at all... but He did. But wait, I am getting ahead of myself.

In August, our church announced a mission trip to Haiti. Peter was immediately inter-ested in going. He just knew it was God's plan for him, even though he had not prayed exten-sively about it. I thought about it

> *And the next event was an event so awful I wouldn't think that God could use it at all... but He did.*

briefly, whispered a quick prayer, then got on the internet and checked it out. I clicked on page after page; the internet laid it out, the words painting the situation in vivid color for me. This is what I found out.

The Bad News

Haiti had experienced a 7.0 catastrophic magni-tude earthquake on January 12, 2010 that devastated it. That was the main reason why our church was going to Haiti. We were going to go and help rebuild homes, bring supplies and help pass out meals. We were going to do whatever they needed done, even though we weren't quite sure what that was.

The epicenter of the earthquake was near Leogane and approximately 16 miles west of Port-au-Prince, Haiti's capital. The Haitian government said that three million people had been affected by the quake: 316,000 people had died, 300,000 were injured and 1,000,000 people had been left homeless. Several experts have questioned the numbers of the death toll, saying it was a guess at best.

The quake was not picky about who it destroyed with its dark hand.

The earthquake happened on January 12th and by January 24,th 52 aftershocks of 4.5 or more magnitude had occurred. Those who still had homes were afraid to sleep indoors.

The quake was not picky about who it destroyed with its dark hand. It chose the pauper as well as the elite to tightly grip with the crush of death. Although, the vast majority of people who died were the poor, many who lived in block houses. The block homes were built with no steel in them or internal support systems. They were built where people could fit them, on slopes, crammed together in small places, mainly on other people's land. There are no building codes in Haiti, and the structures could hardly withstand the ferocious shake dealt them.

Many killed were influential or famous. Among the dead were soccer stars, 30 members of the Federation Haitienne de Football, the Archbishop of Port-au-Prince, Haitian musicians, United Nations personnel including the Missions chief, and the police commissioner. Two hundred unsuspecting guests of the Hotel Montana in Port-au-Prince died, and aid workers and tourists were wiped out too.

Buildings of importance were also affected, destroyed or heavily damaged. The Supreme Court, the Presidential Palace, the National Assembly building, the Port-au-Prince Cathedral and the headquarters for the United Nations Stabilization Mission in Port-au-Prince were all destroyed. The

Prison Civile de Port-au-Prince crumbled, setting 4,000 prisoners free to roam the streets again.

> *The Prison Civile de Port-au-Prince crumbled setting 4,000 prisoners free to roam the streets again.*

The quake seriously damaged the tower at Toussaint L'Ouverture International Airport and the seaport in Port-au-Prince, both of which had to be closed and repaired before reopening. This made it hard for people to immediately get into Haiti to help with medical support and the much needed medical supplies The United States ran the airport for a while and it helped repair the seaport so that it could reopen. The communications infrastructure was terribly damaged too, some cell phone towers, the phone system and radio stations fell silent. People could not communicate well because of this, it was impossible to call to find out where their loved ones were, or if they were safe. All the hospitals in the capital were damaged. Where can you take people for medical care when even the hospitals are in ruins?

Earthquake Damage

The minister of Education Joel Jean-Pierre said that half the nation's schools and three main universities in Port-au-Prince were affected. He lamented that the education system was completely destroyed. More than 1,300 schools and 50 health care facilities were destroyed. After the earthquake it seemed like Haiti had no infrastructure left for the people who lived there.

Reading about all of the losses this country had endured was heartbreaking. Even before this disaster Haiti was overwhelmed with poverty, high unemployment and rampant disease. And now this?

I was there, picturing a sea of dead bodies, smelling the stench of death...

The mass graves that they had to dig to accommodate the dead were chilling. Matie Goldstein, head of the Israeli ZAKA International Rescue Unit delegation to Haiti, described the situation as a form of hell. He compared the thousands of bodies strewn everywhere to holocaust like conditions.

Reading his riveting description made me feel like I was there, picturing a sea of dead bodies, smelling the stench of death that hovered like a dark cloud. It was unnerving! Tears welled up in my eyes and I sat for a minute just staring at the screen.

I clicked off that website and decided to see what the US Department of State had to say about Americans going to Haiti. This is what I read:

The Department of State strongly urges US citizens to avoid travel to Haiti.

JUNE 24, 2010. The Department of State strongly urges US citizens to avoid travel to Haiti. Jan 12, 2010, a 7.0 magnitude earthquake struck close to the nation's capital of Port-au-Prince. Conditions in the area remain hazardous, including extensive damage to buildings, roads, and other infrastructure.

The earthquake significantly reduced the capacity of Port-au-Prince's medical facilities and inadequate public sanitation poses serious health risks.

Strong aftershocks are likely for months after the earthquake.

U. S. citizens traveling to and residing in Haiti despite this warning are reminded that there remains a persistent danger of violent crime, including armed robbery, homicide, and kidnapping. In particular, there have been a number of recent cases in which travelers arriving in Port-au-Prince on flights from the US were attacked and robbed while traveling in cars away from the airport.

> *Police believe criminals may be targeting travelers arriving on flights from the US...*

At least two American citizens have been shot and killed in such incidents in recent months. Police believe criminals may be targeting travelers arriving on flights from the US, following them, and attacking them once they are out of the area.

Most kidnappings are criminal in nature, and the kidnappers make no distinctions of nationality, race, gender or age. Some kidnap victims have been killed, shot, sexually assaulted, or physically abused.

My eyes grew wide when I read the information. We would be staying in Port-au-Prince!

Next, I clicked on the CDC's (Center for Disease Control's) website to find the recommendations for shots. The news wasn't any better. Shot requirements were exhaustive.

Haiti had diseases so terrible I could only remember them as vague horror stories in history...

Haiti has diseases so terrible I could only remember them as vague horror stories in history, like typhoid and anthrax.

"I hate shots!" I thought. The list of diseases mounted, there was HIV, tuberculosis. They even recommended rabies shots. Rabies? I watched a movie called "Old Yeller" as a child and visions of biting animals, foaming at the mouth popped into my head. It made me shutter. I clicked to another website.

Next, I found out that Malaria and Dengue Fever were carried by mosquitoes in Haiti. You had to take a medicine for Malaria even before you left and sometimes, long after you came home to prevent it. You could get one form of Malaria that would not produce any symptoms, until a year later. This, from only a single mosquito bite! Even taking the medicine was not a guarantee of complete safety. There was no cure for Dengue Fever. If you caught it, you just had to let it run its course.

Some internet websites recommended sleeping under mosquito netting injected with mosquito repellent, spraying your skin heavily with an insect repellent with at least 40% DEET and even spraying the clothes you were going to wear before you left for your trip.

Does God Ask You To Do Stupid Things?

"Oh my goodness! I am not going to a place like that!" I thought, turning off the computer. I prayed a short prayer to the Lord, "Unless you tell me specifically to go God, I am NOT going to go there! I don't want to go to a place like that, full of disease, chaos, and danger! If you tell me to go God, you better be really loud because I DON'T WANT TO GO!" God never asks you to do stupid things, does He?

> "If God asks you to do something...kind of weird, don't miss it by turning Him down."

I went to a concert at my sister's church the very next night. Before the music started, Tommy Barnett, a pastor from a large church in Phoenix, got up and spoke a few words to the audience. "If God asks you to do something that is out of your comfort zone and kind of weird, don't miss it by turning Him down. It will change your life. I have seen more people come to the Lord in my 70's than I did the whole first part of my ministry."

"Maybe I will go to Haiti," I thought, his words penetrating my soul like a shaft of light. I woke up the next morning and thought about it. No, I would not go to that awful place. Why would God ask me go somewhere that I didn't want to go? Never once did I think about that little prayer I had prayed so fervently just months before.

Chapter Four: The Seed
Study It!

1. Has God ever asked you to do something strange or uncomfortable? If so, what was it, and what did you do?

2. Read the story in John 21:2-6. Why would God ask us to do things that don't make sense to us?

3. In the prayer of Jabez, (1 Ch 4:10), he prays "Oh, that you bless me indeed, and enlarge my territory, that your hand would be with me, and that you would keep me from evil, that I may not cause pain." (NKJV). If you will pray this prayer, how do you think it will change your own life?

4. Why would God ask you to go somewhere that you didn't want to go?

Chapter 5

TROUBLE ON THE PATHWAY

Have you ever stood in the ocean and felt the stout pull of the waves against your body? As a child I remember standing in the water and being hit by a big wave. Suddenly, my feet came out from under me and I fell toward the sandy ocean floor. In only a few feet of water I could not get up. Struggling with all of my might, I tried to find my footing in the soft sand beneath me, but which direction was it? The strong current which had dunked me, was now holding me under the water with its invisible hand. My toes finally found the ocean floor and with an incredible push, I broke through the wave. Gasping for breath, I gulped in the fresh air with all my might. Pulling against the force of the mighty tide holding me down was a hard task. In fact, in the moment, it felt almost impossible. When God calls you to go anywhere, even if it is just across town, don't be surprised if you encounter resistance. The devil may give you a hard shove or push you down under the circumstances with a powerful force, but get up, and take a deep breath! Even if it feels impossible, get your bearings, stand in faith and think, "This is God's plan, His will for me. He will help me to accomplish it. I *will* overcome!"

Trust in the Lord, even if there is trouble on the pathway.

Therefore put on the full armor of God, so that when the day of evil comes, you may be able to stand your ground, and after you have done everything, to stand.

-Ephesians 6:13 (NIV)

One night in August, Peter had pain in his left side and began running a high fever. "You have appendicitis!" I said. "Please go to the doctor!"

Peter went to the doctor the next morning, and the doctor said, "Unless I don't know my anatomy, you don't have appendicitis. Your stomach should hurt on the right side." I was waiting in the doctor's waiting room, and when Peter came out with an antibiotic and no prescription for a CAT scan, I couldn't believe it.

"He ran a blood test," Peter added when I questioned him. Even though the blood test came back the next day with a high white count the doctor would not relent.

"I think it is diverticulitis, an infection in his bowels," he said when I questioned him the next day on the phone.

Peter did okay for a while, slowly feeling better. We even went to an out of state wedding, but he just wasn't himself. He tired easily, and at night next to me in bed, he felt so hot, like he was on fire.

Soon Peter was staying at home. He could no longer work. He just lay in bed or on the sofa. I took his temperature and found that he was running a high fever that would break to 99 and then go right back up to 101. His stomach began to hurt more, now on the right side.

"I think it is appendicitis," Peter said to me one night while he was lying on the sofa.

I was afraid that Peter would die. I knew he could not wait for this test.

"We have to take you back to the doctor!" I said. This time Peter let me go back with him to see the doctor.

I could tell the doctor still did not believe Peter had appendicitis. "Please doctor, can Peter have a CAT scan of his stomach?" I pleaded. The doctor grudgingly relented, "Okay, but it is not really necessary!" he breathed. He scheduled the CAT scan, but the appointment was not right away. I was afraid that Peter would die. I knew he could not wait for this test. I called another facility and got him an appointment the very next day. On the phone, I asked them if they could read it on the spot and they said yes. The people at the CAT scan place were nice, even after I nervously bumped the container and spilled the thick liquid Peter was required to drink all over their floor. After the test they read it right away just as I had requested.

A Gigantic Crossroad

We could tell something was wrong when they told Peter to sit in the waiting room and not eat or drink anything while they called the doctor.

The lady at the front desk handed the phone to Peter, "You have appendicitis!" the doctor on the other end of the line stammered, "A burst appendix! Who do you want for a surgeon?" Peter didn't answer the doctor, he just handed me the phone in disbelief.

"Who do we want for a surgeon?" he said blankly. I was stunned. I couldn't believe this was really happening.

"Who do we want for a surgeon?" he said blankly. I was stunned. I couldn't believe this was really happening.

"Who do you want for a surgeon?" the doctor

repeated, now to me. Dumbstruck, I had no idea who to use as a surgeon. "Dr. Wright is a good choice," the lady at the front desk offered gently, obviously overhearing the conversation. "He operated on my mother and did a great job."

"We want to have Dr. Wright," I said into the telephone.

"Well, if he is at the hospital, I will see if I can arrange it," the doctor replied. We left the CAT scan office abruptly to head for the hospital.

When we got in the car, we stopped and bowed our heads and prayed.

"Dear God, please help us in this situation. Help us find the right doctor and give him the skill and the wisdom to help us. Amen!"

Dr. Wright was on call at the hospital when we arrived. As we were checking in at the front desk signing papers the lady behind the desk took off her glasses and leaned in across the desk, "Oh, you have Dr. Wright! He operated on my sister! I think he is wonderful!" she said brightly. Those two recommendations, in such a short period of time, by two different people, brought us comfort.

"God has given us a great doctor," I said to Peter as they shuffled him up to a room on the fifth floor of the hospital. In no time at all, a tall doctor with laughing blue eyes walked through the door of Peter's hospital room.

"No surgery?" I questioned. I had never heard of ...a ruptured appendix with no surgery.

"Dr. Wright," he said and held out his hand for Peter to shake and then to me. He felt Peter's stomach, asked a few questions, quickly surveying the situation. Then, he prescribed three antibiotics pills and IV fluid.

"No surgery?" I questioned. I had never heard of anyone having a ruptured appendix without having surgery.

"In ten weeks or so, I will do the surgery," he announced.

Peter didn't flinch. "Can I still go to Haiti on a mission's trip in October?" he exclaimed.

The doctor smiled, his blue eyes crinkling at the corners, "Sure!" he said.

This couldn't be happening! I rolled my eyes. "Come on doctor," I thought loudly, "Are you crazy?"

The doctor turned and left the room as quickly as he had entered.

Then, Peter got on his phone and called our brother-in-law Daryl, who is head of the Emergency Room in a West Virginia hospital, for advice.

This couldn't be happening! I rolled my eyes. "Come on doctor," I thought loudly, "Are you crazy?"

After a long silence on the phone, Daryl replied, "Peter can you find another hospital? This just isn't the plan of action that our hospital would recommend. We would do surgery to remove your appendix right away."

We were left in the dust of a gigantic cross-road. We had prayed for direction and guidance and received Dr. Wright for a doctor. Would we trust the Lord in this situation?

Chapter Five: Trouble on The Pathway
Study It!

1. In chapter five, Jan has a moment in the ocean where she felt like it might be impossible to get up off the ocean floor to catch her breath. Have you ever had a time in your life when you felt like something might be impossible? When? What happened?

2. Read Ephesians 6:11-12. If God asks you to do a task, why might there be trouble ahead for you? Does this mean you are not in God's will? Explain.

3. Have you ever experienced a miracle or seen one happen to someone else? If so, what happened?

4. Why is trusting God so difficult at times?

Chapter 6

T HE PIT OF FEAR

When you set out to follow God with all of your heart, you need to put your flesh and all of its worldly pulls to death. Fear is just one component of your flesh. Fear will try and cage you. Once it has you captured, its nimble fingers will lock your cage, then dangle the key just outside of your reach. Fear will smile at you between the bars, while you stand by, helplessly frozen in place. Sometimes it drifts in little by little, sneaking up on you like a silent marauder. Other times it boldly knocks down your door and grabs you around the throat, choking you with great force.

Fear yells in your face, "Stop! Preserve yourself! God has a crazy plan!" It is the opposite of faith and at times we forget that it cannot be justified. Fear is a deadly enemy and we must stand our ground against it with every ounce of our being. We can use God's word as a sword to slash fear into oblivion.

The Bible tells us that to find your life you have to lose it, (Mt. 10:39). Abandon yourself to God, no matter what the resistance. Trust God and His care for you. Only then, you will get out of the pit, the pit of fear.

For God did not give us a spirit of timidity (of cowardice, of craven and cringing and fawning fear), but (He has given us a spirit) of power and of love, and of calm and well-balanced mind and discipline and self-control.

-2 Tim. 1:7 (AMP)

Miraculously, Peter's body had encapsulated the poison by forming a little pouch around the appendix when it ruptured, instead of pouring it throughout his whole system and killing him.

Even though the poison had been walled off, it had been shedding bacteria in bursts and throwing it into Peter's bloodstream, giving him the high fever.

Now, on the antibiotics the fever stopped. Since his body had walled off the poison, the doctor told him he could do business as usual, except for taking the antibiotics.

I was relieved and grateful to God that Peter was doing so well, but still cautious about Peter's health.

Peter began working almost as hard as usual, driving his tractor on our farm and cleaning up brush and lifting items that I thought were way too heavy to be lifted with a broken appendix! I did not want the pouch to burst open! Why didn't he try harder to take care of himself?

At first I thought there would be no question about it, with his physical condition, surely he would not still want to go to Haiti.

But he popped my bubble soon enough one night, "Janice," he said, "I still think God wants me to go to Haiti." He paused and looked at me pensively, "Why would He call me to go to Haiti and then just change his mind because of circumstances? I feel really conflicted," he continued. "Do I follow God or listen to you? I really feel like I need to follow God's direction over yours." I did not want to believe what I was hearing.

> *"I feel really conflicted," he continued. "Do I follow God or listen to you?"*

"If you are supposed to go to Haiti," I seethed, "then pray and ask God to tell me too!" I was mad at Peter for his stupidity! It is shameful, but I felt mad at God as well, for still asking him to go on this trip with a ruptured appendix. Didn't God know what he had to endure to go to Haiti? I couldn't reason it out in my own head; it just didn't make sense to me.

Even the mission material said, "If you are NOT healthy and cannot endure harsh conditions please do not come." There it was in black and white and Peter still felt God tugging at his heart to go.

Too Heavy To Carry

I asked God how Peter could endure the trip and Haiti with a ruptured appendix. I desperately wanted the answer.

I poured out my heart to Him one day while mowing the lawn, knowing it wasn't logical to get mad at God because He always knows best. He sees the whole picture. He can suspend the natural elements of this world and do things the way He desires.

The Bible even tells us that God's ways are not our ways; they are higher than our ways. But, God's logic was not in my thoughts. I was fighting to get my own way, using my logic, and raw unleashed emotion was spilling everywhere.

I am glad that God is merciful and kind or he could have rubbed me out that very day for my selfish, short-sighted, disrespectful attitude.

Sunday rolled around and morning church. I didn't want to go to church. Somehow, I got ready and went anyway.

I stood as stiff as a soldier in the church. My arms were crossed and my heart was shielded and hard. Then, they started the music. Softly and slowly, like the chords to a beautiful song, the Holy Spirit began to strum on my heart and melt away the hardness. I felt such a pull to give up and let God have his way in Peter's life and mine too. "Lay it all down Janice; it is too heavy," I felt the Holy Spirit's still small voice clearly, "To find your life you must lose it."

"Lay it all down..it is too heavy, to find your life you must lose it."

"You are right, Lord," I thought, the presence of God all around me. My feet followed the path to the altar; the Holy Spirit drew me to my knees. And I cried my heart out. Any thought of being embarrassed at publicly sobbing went out the window. The warm tears ran down my cheeks like a flood, running off all my mascara. My shoulders shook as I sobbed and sobbed. I didn't even care what people might be thinking.

"Whatever you want God, I will obey you. I release my desires, my plans, and my husband to you. Everything is yours anyway, and I have no right to hold onto things I am only borrowing."

> "I will trust you Lord with all of my heart, even if your plan makes no sense to me."

Hadn't I given Jesus my whole life anyway? What was I doing trying to control it myself?

"I will trust you Lord with all of my heart, even if your plan makes no sense to me," I told God.

When I got off my knees at the altar, and stood to go back to my seat, I felt like a vast weight had been lifted from my shoulders. I felt free. No longer was I carrying around the burden of my own way. Enormous peace washed over me and flooded my entire being. With my will squarely set upon the altar, I left it there, and walked away.

I got back to my seat and I grabbed a tissue to wipe my face. That is when an amazing thing happened.

I heard God's voice in my spirit, "Janice, you need to go to Haiti also, not to take care of Peter, but because I have a plan for you!"

> *Then I heard God's voice in my spirit, "Janice you need to go to Haiti ... I have a plan for you!"*

At first I was afraid to tell anyone. I didn't want them to think that I was only going to babysit Peter. I nonchalantly brought it up to Paul the mission trip coordinator after the service, "If someone else decided....I decided," I stammered "to go to Haiti, is it too late?"

"Of course not!" he smiled with a twinkle in his eye. I e-mailed Pastor John the next day and waited for his response.

"Are you going to keep an eye on Peter?" Pastor John asked me.

"No. I am going because I feel like God has a plan for me in Haiti," I typed back. I felt such a great joy when he e-mailed me back telling me that I could go on the trip too! It was a joy that I carried with me from that point, all the way through the trip.

A Critical Decision

But the strangest thing happened to me that Sunday night in my bed after my decision at the altar. In the middle of the night I awoke with a start, terrified; my heart was pounding in my chest so hard I thought it would burst. "You can't go to Haiti!" my mind screamed. "You just can't go!" I felt like jumping out of bed and running through the dark house to get away from the fear. Chill bumps covered my body.

Right then, I knew that I had a decision to make. If I didn't go to Haiti because I was afraid, I could live in fear about everything the rest of my life. The devil could intimidate me right here in America, and he would have won a great stronghold in my life.

No, I would fight the fear! I was going to Haiti! If God can take care of me in America, he can take care of me in Haiti, I told myself. A great peace swept over me, wrapping me like a warm blanket, it enveloped me with the sweetness of God's Holy presence. The fear was gone!

Chapter Six: The Pit of Fear
Study It!

1. Have you ever been paralyzed with fear about a situation? If so, what did you do to overcome it?

2. Why do you think that at first, Jan did not know for sure that God wanted her to go to Haiti?

3. In this chapter, Jan says to God, "I will trust you Lord with all of my heart, even if your plan makes no sense to me." Why was it important for her to give her will to God?

4. Do you ever have trouble listening to God? If so, why?

5. Read 2 Timothy 1:7 How could you use this verse today, to help you overcome fear in your own life?

Chapter 7

IF YOU MAKE YOUR BED IN HELL

On your journey, know that God will be with you! If you go to the darkest jungles of Africa or even just across town to the local high school, He will be there. Take comfort in that thought. Keep it in the front of your heart, always. Even David discovered this simple but powerful truth and expressed it in Psalms when he said, "If I make my bed in hell, even still, you are there."

N ow huddled inside the crowded tap tap our little group was making our way to the base camp where we would be staying for ten days.

Peering through the tiny spaces in the metal cage, the street flicked by. Looking out the back, I could see more of the dusty streets and people. It was night, but people were outside everywhere congregating on the streets. What were they doing?

A huge amount of trash was piled all around, against curbs and gutters, in front of buildings, and in the streets. And earthquake rubble was everywhere!

It felt like I had stepped onto another planet in the back of this strange vehicle with absolutely no rules for driving. Cars and motorcycles were driving like maniacs, including our tap tap. We swayed back and forth against each other sliding on the slick long wooden bench with every move of the vehicle. We were swerving to dodge huge pot holes. Some of them looked like they could swallow a car, or at least tear off a tire or two.

Loud vehicles were passing us on both sides of the truck. Even though most of our view was obstructed by the metal cage of the tap tap, we knew it was a wild ride.

Our bags were piled high on top of the little pickup truck that dutifully followed our tap tap. Some of them were even strapped to the outside of the truck. It was a strange sight.

Even though most of our view was obstructed by the metal cage...we knew it was a wild ride.

Craig was driving so close behind us that I wasn't sure whether he would rear end us or not, as he followed along swerving and slamming on his brakes and accelerating in riotous fashion. People tried to cut in, but he would not allow it. For some reason that made me feel better, more protected.

At a stop light Craig jumped out of his truck. The passenger door flew open, and his passenger jumped out. They ran around circling their truck. What are they doing? A Chinese fire drill? The light changed to green, and they were back inside their truck, they drove on.

Later, we found out that the old man that they had hired to drive our tap tap couldn't really see after dark. Our plane was supposed to be there in the daylight. He had gotten lost on the drive home and circled the airport twice.

After what seemed like thirty minutes, we turned off the pavement and down a dirt road leaving a billowing trail of dust behind us. In another block, we turned down another skinnier dirt road. This road had a huge water filled pothole right in the middle of it. We veered around it slamming into each other on the wooden bench.

The old man they had hired to drive our tap tap couldn't really see after dark.

The road was remote and deserted with high brush on one side and dark buildings on the other. As we slowed to a crawl, we saw a dark spooky building that was partly caved in on one side by the earthquake. Peter looked at me and whispered, "This looks like a place they could rob us and leave us for dead if they wanted to," He winked after he said it.

Shotguns and Razor Wire

The vehicle groaned to a stop just past the caved in building. Our driver jumped out and pulled back a couple of large red steel doors that squealed under the pressure, and we pulled into the compound.

There was a tall block wall around the compound with circles of razor wire atop it. A man with a 12 gauge shotgun stood outside guarding it.

Once inside, we found out that a large Haitian man had broken in four or five times and stolen items, so they had decided to hire the gunman. The last time the man had broken in was two weeks earlier. They had shot at him and missed. He escaped, scaling over the razor wire, leaving a trail of blood behind him, the sharp wire punishing him for his intrusion.

Later, we found that this security system of using guards with shotguns was quite common. Many homes had the same tall block walls with the circles of razor wire atop them for security. Many places were protected by outside gunmen, too.

After hearing about the recent break-in I was thankful for the Haitian man outside that I knew would stay awake all night, guarding our house with his gun.

Razor wire on the wall above the foliage

Be Prepared For Anything

This would be our new home for ten days instead of two man tents like we were told before we left on the trip. In this house we would be staying divided, men and women, in bunk beds, dormitory style.

I felt relieved, yet a bit disappointed. Peter and I had packed many of our toiletries together, one tube of tooth paste, one bottle of shampoo. How were we going to divide that stuff? Besides that the romance of staying in a tent with Peter was inviting. In reality, I knew staying in the house was a better proposition by far.

The house was a nice two story block home with white squared ceramic tile floors. The court yard around the house was full of exotic plants, palm trees and pretty flowers. Of course, we didn't see this in the dark when we arrived.

"We need to have an orientation," Craig said as soon as we got inside. We each took a seat in the living room settling down on the worn rattan furniture with faded flowers. Our host came in and greeted us warmly. His gentle face framed with white wavy hair and dark blue eyes was welcoming. After his initial greeting, he went over the list of house rules.

"You must be quiet after 9pm. Men use the bathroom downstairs, the women the one upstairs." He went on with his short list. Then he changed the subject.

What he said next, I was completely unprepared for. His tone changed and his face became grim, "A hurricane is barreling right towards us. Right now the hurricane is set for a direct hit on Port-au-Prince in two days. If it hits here, it will be a disaster! With all the people in tents and all the rubble and disease, we cannot afford to have a hurricane hit this area." I could see the compassion in his face as he spoke. He truly loved these people. "Please pray that this will not happen! Maybe that is why God sent your team here... to pray." His voice trailed off and he turned and walked out of the room.

What he said next I was completely unprepared for, his tone changed and his face became grim.

Right before we arrived, it was announced there was a cholera outbreak and now a hurricane!

This unsettling news was so horrible, I almost wanted to laugh. How many things could the devil use against this place?

My mind began to wander to what it would be like to have a hurricane hit the mission compound. Shattered blocks caving in all around us, the ravaging wind whipping over the grounds, dumping loads of water, I could easily picture it. Or worse yet, for the hurricane to slam into the masses of people living in flimsy tents on the steep hillsides. Surely, the tents would be smashed and ripped apart. Then the rushing water would cause mud slides, and the tents would be washed down the deep ravines, destroying every soul caught in the hurricane's path. I didn't want to imagine it. One thing was for sure, there was no running away for now. We would be here in two days, hurricane or not. We would just have to pray; there was no other option. I knew God was able to change the hurricane's path, if only we would believe.

It was dinner time, so we lined up for dinner single file in the kitchen, plastic plates in hand taken from the stack laid on the long wooden table.

Filing past the pots of prepared food, I could see that dinner was in two pots. In one pot was some sort of chunky looking chicken floating in bright orange gravy. Right next to it was a second pot, a big silver pot, of macaroni and cheese with tiny red peppers in it. I skipped the chicken and strange looking gravy and opted for the familiar, the macaroni and cheese. It was already cold.

While lined up in the kitchen the lights suddenly went out. It was total blackness...

While lined up in the kitchen the lights suddenly went out. It was total blackness; you couldn't even see your hand in front of your face. I had a moment of panic in the suffocating darkness. Then, after an eternity, which really was only seconds, Craig opened his cell phone and a tiny glow filled the room.

"Ka-chink," the electric kicked back on. We found out that the electric there was very spotty.

They had "street power" and "generator power". Just before we came, we learned that they had gone eighteen consecutive days without "street power." The fans could not be run in the day if there was no street power because it was too expensive to run the generator in the day and night too. It was oppressively hot and humid in the house without the fans, but not completely unbearable. At night, the girls had a small window air conditioner that functioned okay most nights, but did not make it really cool.

One night it shut itself off in the middle of the night. We woke up drenched the next morning.

We did have two big fans that sat in the middle of the room. Each fan rotated back and forth between its set of beds to stir up a breeze. This helped a lot. Just when you thought you would not be able to stand the heat any longer, the fan would turn and blow in your face. We felt blessed because it was a world of difference over what the men had, with no air conditioning.

We slept in wooden bunk beds covered with mosquito netting. When I first crawled inside the netting, I could picture all of those exotic movies where they slept with mosquito netting over their beds. It was exhilarating! My own little space in a dorm full of women!

I picked a bottom bunk as did Charity and Michelle. Rachel, a twenty something girl who worked for the base camp, already had her bottom bunk staked out when we arrived. Ariel and Macrae opted for the top bunks. I was thankful that I wouldn't be climbing up and down those stairs on the side of the bed in the middle of the night.

The sign on the bathroom wall read us the rules, "If it is yellow, let it mellow, if it is brown, flush it down".

The Rules

We had one bathroom for our group of six women. The men had one bathroom for nine men plus the other men at the base camp which totaled seventeen men. We found out later that some of the men (staff) snuck in and used ours. We were not allowed to flush the toilet, most of the time. The sign on the bathroom wall read us the rules, "If it is yellow, let it mellow, if it is brown, flush it down."

No toilet paper was allowed in the toilet. It was to be piled next to the toilet in a trash can. I could hardly stand to glance at the trash can full of soiled paper. This felt so barbaric to me. I hated leaving the bathroom without flushing the toilet. I hated how my hands felt washing them in unclean water. Peter had a totally different opinion of the situation.

"We don't even have to put down the seat!" he said with glee when we discussed the bathroom rules.

That night we had our first prayer and praise service, which we would continue to have every night. Pastor John led the prayers and one of the guys from the base camp played his guitar, and we sang songs. That night the Spirit of God was very strong in the little living room. The peace of God settled over each one of us.

I slept very well that night in my bottom bunk, even though every time I moved, the wooden board under my feet squeaked.

Chapter Seven: If You Make Your Bed In Hell Study It!

1   Jan talks about the bathroom situation. Have you ever been on a trip with a bathroom circumstance that made you uncomfortable? Share it!

2   Read Psalms 139:8b "If I make my bed in hell, behold, You *are there.*" What does that mean to you?

3   In this chapter Jan describes some hair- raising events that happened when she first entered Haiti. Have you ever experienced an event in your life that challenged you? Describe how, or if, you trusted God.

4   How does it change us to know that God is always with us no matter where we go? Explain.

Chapter 8

HOPELESSNESS

Discouragement is an evil pest. It can come at any point in your life. It can hit you like a load of bricks or roll in like fog, quietly creeping over the valley, settling in the low places first, until it covers the entire landscape. It can completely obscure your view of life and will seep into any crack you let it in. This usually means victory is just around the corner. If you will realize this is just an attack from the enemy to dissuade you, you will be ahead of the game! You will overcome mightily when discouragement knocks on your door with its companion, hopelessness.

Sunday met us bright and early the next morning. I got out of bed and put on my pink fan skirt and a pair of boots to go to church. I picked up a lot of my clothes at Goodwill before I left, so I could leave them in Haiti.

At home I thought boots would be a good choice of shoes to wear walking in the dusty conditions. Everyone else seemed to have brought nice looking church shoes. A couple of people snickered at the way I looked with the skirt and the boots, but I didn't really care.

We walked a block on the dusty gravel road to the church. It was only a tin roof with metal chairs sitting underneath it. They had built a stage beneath the roof too, to play their instruments and do the preaching. The church building had been completely destroyed by the earthquake.

Now, in its place was a slab of concrete that they had poured a couple weeks before in anticipation of a metal building that was yet to be delivered, still waiting in customs. In the stifling heat, I figured that an open air church was probably best anyway, perhaps there would be a breeze.

I greeted several Haitians in Creole, eager to practice the language that I had learned from the internet. "Koman ou ye?" (How are you?) They did not seem very impressed. Maybe I had pronounced it wrong. They smiled at me warily.

> *I greeted several Haitians with the Creole words I had learned from the internet...they did not seem very impressed.*

The rest of the team seemed to keep their distance. It felt awkward. Some of the people glanced over, eyeing us during the service. I wondered what they were thinking.

I had written a script using the colors of the Christian wordless book, explaining the plan of salvation, and George had recorded it in his native tongue of Creole before we left for Haiti.

Even though I didn't really know George at the time and had only talked to him once on the phone, he had gladly met me at my church and recorded it. Now, the Haitian people could hear the plan of salvation in their own language. I found a great price on five tee shirts, and we came up with actions for each tee shirt color. There were a lot of problems getting the recording to its final stage. My brother Carl graciously recorded the finished product on his professional equipment. Finally it was complete and well done.

> *I asked Paul if we could give the gospel presentation that we had brought and he went to ask. It was a go!*

I asked Paul if we could give the gospel presentation that we had brought and he went to ask. It was a go! We had never even practiced it yet. I wasn't sure how to handle the gospel presentation in the church. I created it to be enacted on the street, not in the church. The last part of the recording talked about giving out pamphlets and asked the people to attend that church. God worked it out.

Almost at the end of the tape, Elder who was only suppose to mime his part, began speaking, telling the people they could ask Jesus into their heart and the guy running the tape switched it off. I was sure that Elder had not known about the dilemma. Jesus is in control! We had not even discussed it.

Dramatic Presentation: Michelle wearing the red shirt

The church service was hot and long. There was no breeze. I was so hot and sweaty that I wanted to fan myself, but I didn't dare. No one else was fanning themselves. Weren't they hot? I looked around and no one else even looked sweaty.

It was youth Sunday and a young man named Emmanuel got up to address the audience. Looking sharp in his brown suit he began preaching in Creole. The pastor of the church stood on the platform next to him ready to interpret it into English for our team. Passionately, Emmanuel poured out his heart to us through the interpreter, " Being a Christian is hard, but don't ever give up!" It was a good sermon and I figured that living in Haiti life was pretty hard, whether you were a Christian or not.

A Haitian girl at the end of the aisle passed a tiny baby down the row like an offering basket.

A Haitian girl at the end of the aisle passed a tiny baby down the row like an offering basket. The small baby stopped in the lap of Michelle who was sitting next to me. Even though it was hot, the baby was wrapped in a blanket. She was positively beautiful with perfect features, but she was the tiniest child I had ever seen! I was amazed.

"Do you want to hold her?" Michelle whispered to me.

"No thanks," I said. I felt too hot and sweaty to hold this fragile, little angel. After the service we found out that the baby's mother had died in child birth only a few days before. Her friend was left to care for the baby.

This is where we first met Geraldo, a sixteen year old Haitian boy who lived in the small camp next door to the church. He was an outgoing, handsome kid who was tall and thin with a broad smile. During worship he stood as others sat, his eyes closed his hands raised to heaven as he worshipped the Lord.

After the service, he approached Ariel and Macrae whom he had been glancing at off and on during the message, "You girls are beautiful, the most beautiful girls I have ever seen!" He cooed.

We talked to a few other people and then our group made our way back to the base camp.

The Tent Camp

Our lunch of salami, ham and cheese on stale white bread could have been a Haitian feast, as many do not get enough to eat. Rodney took note of this and often gave his granola bars to Haitians that we met along the way.

After lunch we took a walk with Craig who was our guide for the week. Craig was a tall guy and very broad shouldered. He looked like the type of guy who would be hired to be a bouncer in a rough bar or a body guard of some sort. He was our body guard, our guide, companion and friend. We grew to love and respect this mighty man of God who took such great care of us.

Some of the men left with our host to scope out the building project for the next day. They were going to build a house for a woman in the church. Craig described the location as a town that could take 30 minutes to get to on a good day or 3 hours on a bad day, depending on the traffic.

"Stay close to me and don't take pictures or make eye contact with the people" Craig commanded us.

"Do you want to go on a walk and see a tent camp?" Craig had asked the rest of us after the other group had left. Of course we did!

Walking to the tent camp with Craig, we cut through a field with a skinny dirt path that had been well traveled. It had tall bushes and weeds on either side that hung over the path.

"Stay close to me and don't take pictures or make eye contact with the people," Craig commanded us.

Sickening smells hit us in waves, as we picked our way down the skinny, dirt path, avoiding the piles of human feces we occasionally encountered. In some places brush completely obscured the path. The camp had little tents and shanties built with patched together tin. Some people were standing outside and watched us carefully. I tried to obey and not look back at them.

A couple of little kids ran up to hug Craig. He was a big guy and could look very imposing, but underneath you could see love in his face when he hugged the children.

Along the way, we saw a pig eating a pile of trash and a skinny donkey that looked like a bag of bones. I wondered if they were pets or if they would be used for food.

We saw a small stream which ran by some palm trees. "This is where the people come to wash their clothes," Craig said. "They also use it as their drinking water," he continued. "Really? Their only source of water?" I asked. It looked more like a large puddle, than a stream.

Relieved to finally make it through the camp, I had no idea that later that camp would make a significant impact on my life.

When we got back the heat had taken its toll. Looking in the mirror I discovered my face was bright red. It had only been a thirty minute trip! Charity and Michelle were lying in their bunks with red faces, too.

They both complained of pounding heads. Wondering how I could help them cool down, I searched the kitchen downstairs and brought them the only ice I could find, which was "dirty ice." It was keeping the soda bottles cool. I found some plastic baggies and stuffed in the ice. I didn't realize at the time, but I was pretty overheated too.

Later that evening they asked if we wanted to go to the youth service. "The youth service?" I was hot and tired, and I didn't feel much like going. Everyone else on the team was going, so I went too. I didn't want to miss a drop of what God had for me in Haiti!

The Youth Service

...their faces were glowing with joy. How could it be that many of them had nothing but tents to live in?

When we arrived, we were warmly greeted by fifteen or so Haitian teenagers, who were completely in charge of their own service. There were no other adults present, other than in our group.

We were not in the area where we had met for the main church service, but now we were outside next to that area with a circle of metal chairs set up in the dirt.

The kids tried hard to incorporate us into the service so that we would feel a part of it. We sang songs about Jesus. We clapped in patterns, we repeated the words "Bonswa" (Good afternoon) and "Salute," which I had no idea of the meaning. We really bonded with the Haitian teens. The happy Haitian kids had the warmest smiles, their faces were glowing with joy. How could it be that many of them had nothing but tents to live in and not enough food to eat?

Night was falling, and a gentle breeze was blowing as we returned to the base. By now I felt bone tired.

> "What is that?" I asked Charity who was standing behind me. "I am not sure," she said, peering into the pot and making a face.

Dinner was ready when we got back. That night they were serving black beans and rice with lettuce, onion and tomato on the side.

When I first approached the pot of beans, I wasn't sure what dish it was. It was not very eye pleasing. Haitians take the black beans and crush them with spices until it is a black runny sauce, they leave a few whole beans, but the majority of the beans are completely crushed in the sauce.

"What is that?" I asked Charity who was standing behind me.

"I am not sure," she said, peering into the pot

and making a face. I scooped a little bit of white rice on my plate and my appetite left me. Spooning a small amount of the black mess onto my rice just to taste it, I moved on. Not being an adventuresome food connoisseur, I took a very small portion. After I tasted it at the table I regretted not taking more of it.

"This is really good!" I said to Peter.

"I know!" he smiled back licking his spoon.

"The next time they serve this I will make sure to take more," I whispered.

"Yuck!" Frank sputtered. "This fruit takes like vomit!"

This did not prove true of the fresh papaya that they served at breakfast every day. People either love or hate papaya, there isn't much of a middle ground. I had tasted it years before and wasn't about to get any of that stuff. Frank piled a bunch on his plate and with great anticipation bit into a chunk.

"Yuck!" Frank sputtered. "This fruit tastes like vomit!" Rodney had the fruit mounded on top of his oatmeal. "You are crazy man! I love this fruit, especially when the juice mixes with my oatmeal," Rodney said. Papaya was also one of Pastor John's favorite fruit too.

That night at our little prayer and praise service the base group leader told us the projects for the week. They were all building projects.

I wondered why God had brought me here.

It was too dangerous to go out at night; we could not go anywhere to minister to the people and all there was to do was help build things. I wondered why God had brought me here.

I felt dirty and hot. You could not brush your teeth with the water, but could wash in it. After a shower with dirty water you had to apply mosquito spray loaded with DEET to your body and chemical hand cleaner filled with drying alcohol to your hands. I blurted out to Charity, "I feel like I am camping! I feel so dirty!" Earlier I had told her how much I hated camping.

On the way up to bed, I met Peter on the stairs

to say good night. "I don't know why God brought me to Haiti. There is nothing that I can do here," I muttered.

"Do you think you missed God?" he said.

"Maybe," I said with tears rolling down my face. He gave me a hug. "Oh great woman of faith you are," I thought sarcastically. I got in bed and quietly cried some more, thankful for the privacy of the mosquito net.

I prayed that God would have people in America pray for me. "Maybe my mom would be praying for me tonight." I hoped. What did I get myself into? I wondered.

Chapter Eight: Hopelessness
Study It!

1. How can discouragement change your life?

2. The author confesses that she is, "not an adventure-some food connoisseur." Are you? Explain your answer.

3. In chapter 8, Jan again struggles with her purpose for being in Haiti. Analyze why she did that. Do you ever struggle with your purpose?

4. Read Isaiah 55:8-10. How does understanding that God's ways are different from our ways help us?

Chapter 9

Aplan for me

Expect God to use you! This may sound silly. Why wouldn't you? But sometimes people miss opportunities because they don't see them. If you expect that God will bring opportunities to you, you are constantly looking for them. Listen carefully to the Holy Spirit and wait for Him to point something or someone out to you that you might otherwise miss. Be ready to step into any situation that awaits you, armed with the power of His Spirit. It is not self importance to think that God has a plan for you and that He has exact things for you to do. God wants to use you to touch and change others lives for His glory. This is God's plan. The things that He accomplishes with His Spirit will be lasting. Just think to yourself, "God has a plan for me!"

The morning light came streaming in the barred window and woke me up. I lay in the bed and quietly cried some more. Then, I blew my nose and went down stairs. I decided that I wouldn't even wear makeup that day which was out of character for me. "It will only melt off my face anyway," I thought. "Who cares?"

Peter greeted me at the bottom of the stairs with a happy good morning and told me how good I looked. In that moment, in the light of that compliment, I put all of the despair behind me and decided that this was a new day.

After a breakfast of a slim fast bar and pineapple, (everyone else ate Haitian oatmeal), our host told us the plans had changed. We realized that this happened a lot, and we should just be flexible. "God's plans always get accomplished if we trust in Him," I told myself.

Plans For A Belt

I thought about Chuck's belt. Peter had told me the story about it that morning. When Chuck went to put on his belt yesterday morning it came apart in his hands, breaking into two pieces. He was a bit concerned because without this belt his pants would not stay up.

"Hey Rodney, do you have anything I can sew my belt up with?" Chuck moaned clearly in distress about what he was going to do to keep up his pants. For some strange reason Peter had packed two belts to go to Haiti. He wasn't sure why he did it; he just threw in an extra one at the last minute. When Peter found out about Chuck's dilemma he gave Rodney his extra belt.

"Don't tell him where you got the belt," Peter said. Later, Rodney handed Chuck the belt. Relief flooded Chuck's face as he put it on.

"Hey thanks, Rodney. This belt fits perfectly! Is this your belt?"

"Not my belt!" Rodney said truthfully.

"Whose belt is it?" Chuck inquired. Chuck looked around the room, trying to figure out who would have given him their belt.

"Is it your belt Peter?"

"My belt is right here, Chuck," Peter said, pulling up his shirt and patting the belt he was wearing. Chuck was perplexed. A bunch of pastors were also bunking with the men. They had just arrived.

Chuck didn't know what to believe,... grateful for the belt holding up his pants. He was sure God had provided it for him.

"Tell Chuck that you took a belt that was hanging on the bunk of the pastor from Hawaii to give to him and left the broken one in its place" Peter joked. They even hung the broken belt on the pastor's bed post and asked the Hawaiian pastor to tell Chuck that his belt looked a lot like the one that Chuck had on.

"No," I guess it isn't my belt the Hawaiian pastor joked, "but it looks so similar!"

"Really?" Chuck said confused. Chuck didn't know what to believe, but he was very grateful for the belt holding up his pants. He wasn't sure which person had given him the belt, but he was sure that God had provided it for him. After the trip Peter confessed it was his belt and that God had him pack an extra one. "He goes before us and comes up with the things we need before we need them doesn't He?" Chuck smiled.

"He sure does!" Peter said cheerfully. This incident made a major impact on Chuck. When we got home from Haiti and shared about our experience in front of the church, Chuck brought it up again.

"I just couldn't believe how God had provided for me!" he said.

Voodoo Holidays Mean Changed Plans

In the changed plans, the men would not be going to get the supplies to build the home today because it was a Voodoo holiday and all the stores with the building materials would be closed. November 1& 2 are called, "All Saints Day" and "All Souls Day" respectively.

Voodoo is a mixture of African spiritualism and witchcraft. Voodoo legend says that on these days the Guede Loa (demon spirits) come out of the cemeteries, possess their horses and come into the hounforts (homes) to amuse themselves. On August 8, 2003, President Jean-Bertrand Aristide approved

Voodoo as an officially recognized religion in Haiti. Voodoo priests can now perform marriages and other ceremonies previously reserved for the Christians to perform.

I thought back to what George and Florence had told us about the history of Haiti while we were sitting in the ice cream store.

Satan's Plan

"Some people will deny it," he said, "But the nation of Haiti was dedicated to Satan 200 years ago".

"What?" I said. I felt chills run down my back.

"Some Voodoo priests led by a former slave came together and made a covenant with the devil. It was at Bois-Caiman, a mountain in Haiti. The slaves did not want to be ruled by the French. Thirsty for their freedom, they unanimously vowed to kill every Frenchman on the island. They wanted to make this demonic pact an official public ceremony so they concocted an eerie Voodoo ceremony where a spirit possessed a voodoo priestess. Then, in this evil ritual they sacrificed a black pig and hundreds of the slaves drank the pig's blood to seal the pact. In this ritual, they asked Satan for his help in defeating the French and freeing Haiti from the French's reign. In exchange, they promised to serve Satan and give him the country for 200 years.

The Frenchmen were supernaturally defeated. Many of the French grew sick with no explanation and the much smaller band of Haitians soundly trounced them."

George continued unraveling this incredible story as we sat transfixed, "On January 1, 1804, the nation of Haiti was born. That is when Satan began his new reign of terror."

George continued unraveling this incredible story before us as we sat transfixed, "On January 1, 1804, the nation of Haiti was born. That is when Satan began his new reign of terror. Before the pact with the devil, Haiti was France's richest colony, and was known as the 'Pearl of the Antilles' for its beauty and richness. But, overnight it became one of the world's poorest and most blighted nations because the people had given themselves and their country to Satan."

We could see how Haiti had once been a pearl;

underneath all of the poverty and pain you could see glimmers of great beauty, in the people, in the foliage and the mountains.

> "Until a new leader arises, he said ... and breaks this contract with the devil in a public ceremony, things will not change."

"Until a new leader arises," he said, his eyes shining with determination, "and breaks this contract with the devil in a public ceremony, things will not change." He paused. "This leader must break the contract with the devil and make a new agreement with the Lord Jesus."

As I thought back over his words, I wondered if one of the young people we had met in the open air church service could possibly be that leader. Peter had felt like Jesus was standing beside him during the Sunday service and telling him, "This is the future of Haiti!" Maybe this was why.

Distribution Plans

Now the plan was to go through the mound of

the things that we brought to the people of Haiti. We dumped our suitcases, which were groaning with supplies, in the downstairs living room and sorted through them for distribution. We put the children's clothes together by sizes, sorted the toys, and bagged the hygiene items, labeling them as we went.

Later, we filled backpacks we had brought with toys and hygiene items for the orphanage children.

Be His Hands & Feet & Ears?

Afterwards, Michelle, Charity and I sat on the couch and talked. "God told me that we should walk in His Spirit. We should be his hands and feet and ears and walk out His plan," Michelle said. "I was going to share this with the group tonight, but I thought I would tell you right now." This word really touched my heart, it changed my thinking and the direction of what I thought God wanted me to do in Haiti.

"Hmmm, be His hands, His feet, His ears?" As we sat there I wished with all my heart that we could pray for someone, but we weren't allowed to go and minister on the streets to anyone because of the danger.

I looked around and saw one of the house girls, Louisa across the room in the kitchen. She reminded me of a ballet dancer, she was very thin with a slight frame and a gracefulness about her. She was mopping all the floors today. I felt a bit ashamed. Here she was mopping all the floors while we sat on the sofa.

"Do you want to pray for the house help?" I asked the Michelle and Charity. Without waiting for them to answer, I got up and approached Louisa. I asked her if she wanted us to pray for her.

"Yes!" she said, as she threw her arms around my neck and hugged me tightly.

"Are you sick?" I asked.

"Yes!" she said and held her stomach. I don't know if she really understood or not, but we each laid a hand on her back and began to pray for her.

"Thank you!" She said smiling, her face aglow when we were finished. She seemed to really appreciate it. A bit later we asked the other house girl, Linda, who was cleaning the bathroom if she wanted prayer. She, too, said yes. Michelle and I prayed for her. I felt God's presence.

This was one of the reasons we came to Haiti, to pray! We sat in the living room and prayed for the base camp, the country, and the team. It was a wonderful time.

Later that afternoon we were told the men were going back to the tent camp to build a shelter. Earlier, they had dismantled one because it was built on property that was just sold. "Do you girls want to go and play with the kids?" Craig asked.

> *This was one of the reasons we came to Haiti, to pray!*

"And give out candy?" I added. Yes, we could do that.

I asked how long we would be gone and Craig said, "Four hours".

Four hours? Yikes! Yesterday, I had trouble in the heat with a half an hour walk, as did some of the others. I was a little embarrassed, but I asked Craig if he could bring me back early if it was too hot.

Without hesitation he cheerfully agreed to do that.

New Playmates!

When we pulled into the camp, it was full of children. They were all different ages. Some of them were dirty and one little boy had a shirt with no pants on. Another child was wearing a shirt and a pair of white underwear. No matter what they had or didn't have on physically, these little kids were all dressed in bright smiles. They were clearly happy to see their new playmates.

No matter what they had or didn't have on physically, these little kids were all dressed in bright smiles.

The men began the structure, and the rest of us played with the kids.

Armed with my hat and sunglasses to combat the bright sun, I had a soccer ball to give away. Peter had bought the ball specifically for that purpose.

Geraldo, the 16 year old that we had met at the Sunday service approached us when we arrived. He smiled brightly when he saw us.

Here was a kid who had no video games, no TV, whose whole family lived in a one room tent with no bathroom or clean water, no light switch to flip for electricity, and not even enough food to eat, yet he knew God's purpose for his life.

"Hello," he said. We spent several minutes talking. "My mission," he confessed to me during our conversation "is to spread the gospel. That is my purpose!" Wow! I couldn't imagine any of the 16 year olds I knew saying that. Here was a kid who had no video games, no TV, whose whole family lived in a one room tent with no bathroom or clean water, no light switch to flip for electricity, and not even enough food to eat, yet he knew God's purpose for his life. Who is really better off in the long run? I thought to myself. Aren't we supposed to live our lives in the light of eternity? This kid was doing just that. I looked down at the soccer ball,

"Would you like to have this ball when we are

done playing with it?" I asked him.

"Oh yes!" he exclaimed, but soon he disappeared when his friends arrived. "I'll be back mama!" he smiled calling behind him. That is what he called all of us mothers.

We played with twenty-five or so kids that afternoon. We kicked the soccer ball with the children, running up and down the dusty little corridor they used as a playground.

One little boy looked surprised when I kicked the ball right through his legs and ran past him. I could almost hear him thinking, "How did *she* do that?"

We played "Ring around the Rosie," as well as, "Patty Cake" and the game where you challenge the person to try and hit your hands. You had to be quick to move your hands when the children would slap down on them or else you received a tremendous sting. I made sure to yelp pretty good when they caught me. It added to their fun. Yelping is the same in any language!

Charity was busy snapping pictures of the children playing. They gathered around her to see her camera, begging for more photos!

Me, Singing in Creole?

George had taught me a song in Creole. I recorded him singing it and made a CD of it that I played over and over while driving in my car. I would sing at the top of my lungs with George on the CD, oblivious to the eyes of the other drivers around me.

The work had paid off. I was able to sing the song in Creole, "I am so Happy Jesus Loves Me!" I sang loudly. I pretended to have a microphone in my hand, switching it from child to child so they could sing into it too. The kids caught on quick; they knew the song just like George said they would. They joined in the pretend game and sang along smiling and giggling. I told them over and over again "Jesus loves you!" in their native language. I told them so many times, I expected them to hear it in their sleep that night. We hugged them and held them, and they loved the affection.

Chuck stopped working for a minute and came over to get a drink of water. The children surrounded him and he flipped his false teeth around in his mouth for the children to see, and they loved it. Wide-eyed, they broke out in smiles, giggling. He did it again and again, and finally, he had to go back to work. I could imagine how magical it seemed to them. I bet they had never even heard of false teeth! To them it was probably like flipping real teeth upside down.

Chuck stopped working for a minute...he flipped his false teeth around in his mouth for the children to see and they loved it.

I looked over and saw that Ariel was being bombarded with children; they were crawling all over her, hanging off of her back and draping themselves over her arms.

Craig was chasing a little boy with a ball, trying to kick it away from him. The little boy made a quick stop and turned and kicked it to other child. Craig stopped and put his hands on his hips, out of breath

Then, Ariel and Macrae decided to make a circle with the kids. They all grabbed hands and it was "Ring Around The Rosie." Again!

I glanced over at the men. They were huddled together working hard on building the open structure. The church had planned to do Bible lessons from it and use it as a place to help the people of the little camp. It was about a '10 x 10' area, constructed by digging four holes in the ground and then cementing four posts into the ground. Last, they added a thin metal roof with pieces of tin as a covering.

Later, I stopped and looked over to see how well the structure was coming along. Paul was sitting on one side of a beam and Randy on the other, way up in the sky. They were each being held up in the air by a thin wooden beam. Each man was balancing himself in mid air, working to finish the shelter. I thought what a disaster it would be if a child accidently shook the structure or if either one of the men had weighed more, or had less balance.

Four hours later, they were done. I had not gotten too hot or too tired; in fact, I felt energized!

Right before we left, Craig had the children make a line and we gave each one a piece of candy. My heart would break each time a child would ask me for food.

My heart would break every time a child would ask me for food. "Food! Food!" they would say, holding their little stomachs."

"Food! Food!" they would say, holding their little stomachs. I wished we could have given them food. We knew they were hungry and to give them only a couple pieces of candy seemed shameful, but it was all we had, all we were allowed. I knew that there was a better way to feed them and also, that the church was working very hard on the solution already.

God's Plan

Michelle and I prayed for some of the people. We prayed for many of the children, laying our hands on their heads or holding them in our arms.

One little boy took my hand and led me up to a small tin shack where a woman I assumed was his mother was holding a baby that looked about one year old. I wondered if the baby was sick. Michelle followed as we approached the lady; she burst into a wide welcoming smile. We bowed our heads and touched her arm gently and began to pray for her. When we finished, I opened my eyes and she handed me her baby. The baby stiffened in my arms, not sure who I was, but soon relaxed as I began praying softly for her. The grateful mother again smiled at me. She knew no English but her eyes communicated perfectly.

She knew no English, but her eyes communicated perfectly.

Suddenly another little boy was grabbing me around the waist trying to pull himself up into my arms. He wanted to be held. I scooped him up, and then at the same time, a small child had his arms around my legs hugging them tightly. Michelle grasp the child hanging onto my legs and picked him up, drawing him close. We prayed for them.

I approached two young men standing together and spoke to them in English. A few of the people knew English and these boys did. "Can I pray for you?" I asked. "What are your requests?"

"I want to be able to finish my education," the first young man said, "to be able to go to college." Education is not free in Haiti. People must pay to go to school, and money is scarce. Unemployment is 80%.

"And what would you like God to do for you?"...I was touched by his prayer request.

"God sent me from America to pray for you," I wanted him to know. After his prayer, I was left with the other young man. "And what would you like God to do for you?" I asked looking into his eyes. I was touched by his prayer request. He opened up his heart to me and shared his deepest desire.

"Ask," Jesus said, "and it will be given unto you"...with simple faith I was asking.

"I want to see my Father," he said. I could see the yearning in his eyes. "He lives far away. I don't know where he is. I want to find him. Please pray for me." I didn't really fully understand the situation, but I knew that the God, who knows how many hairs are on each of our heads, did. I prayed for him and knew that God would answer his request.

This is why God sent me from America. God wanted to do amazing things! He wanted the people of Haiti to know that He loved them. He wanted to show them in a mighty way that He had not forgotten them. Why else would He have sent me, an ordinary person, who had strongly resisted His call to come all of this way, if He did not have a great purpose?

We prayed for a few other adult men standing around, some could not tell us their requests, but God knew each one of their needs.

It was the work He wanted done. "Ask" Jesus

said, "and it will be given unto you." "For everyone who asks receives…" (Matthew 7:7-8). With simple faith I was asking, knowing that God who is all powerful and all knowing would answer the prayers and intervene in the situations as only He can. When we left the camp my feet could hardly touch the ground. I was so full of joy. Yes, God did have a plan for me in Haiti!

Chapter Nine: A Plan For Me
Study It!

1. How could expecting God to use you every day, make a difference in your life?

2. Read John 10:10. Do you think Satan has a plan for you? Why or why not?

3. In this chapter, what happened to make Jan aware that God did have a plan for her?

4. How can thinking that God doesn't have a plan for you affect your life?

5. Why was Chuck's belt significant to this story?

Chapter 10

THE ORPHANAGE

I once heard a story about an old man walking on a sea shore throwing starfish back into the ocean that the tide had left stranded on the beach. A young man standing on the beach approached the old man, "Mr., don't you know that you can't save all of these starfish?" he chided, "You are making no difference at all, why look on the sand, there are hundreds of starfish on the beach that are dying."

The old man looked up with a gleam in his eye. Cocking his head to one side, he exclaimed "I am making all the difference in the world to this starfish." And then he turned and flung the starfish that he had just picked up back into the ocean.

Stepping out for God, can sometimes be a lot of trouble. At times you have to plan and prepare. It can be expensive. It costs your time and your money. But if you can make a difference in even one person's life, it will be worth it. Maybe somebody will be in heaven someday because you were obedient to do what God wanted you to do. You will make a difference for the glory of God, even though you may never know what that difference was.

This morning Louisa was busy at the little outdoor stove making breakfast in a big kettle. It was Haitian oatmeal. This time I decided to try the blend of oatmeal and cornmeal with a cinnamon stick in it. The doubts I had about the strange mixture disappeared in my first bite. Mmmm! It tasted better than any oatmeal that I had ever eaten. We also had a delightful array of bananas, mangos and papayas to enjoy. Why hadn't I eaten it before?

Because it was the second day of the holiday all the lumber stores were still closed, Craig decided to take us to the orphanage in the mountains. I didn't know what to expect at the orphanage.

Before we left, I had gotten online and read some blogs about some of the orphanages in Haiti. There are thousands of orphans in Haiti. After the earthquake, I am sure that number has skyrocketed.

A few of the blogs I read about some of the orphanages in Haiti were unsettling. One reported deplorable conditions like raw sewage overflowing from a port-a-potty just outside one of the windows of the orphanage. The smell was so bad the children often had trouble sleeping. There were disgusting unsanitary floors and no utensils for the kids to eat or drink with, they were using dirty bottles found in the trash to drink from.

My nose is as sharp as any bloodhound's nose which detects even the faintest smell. I didn't know how I would react if I found heart breaking conditions at this orphanage. I tossed those thoughts far behind me as I rode in the air conditioned cab which sealed out the smell of the streets, the coolness a treat from the scorching heat.

> *I didn't know how I would react if I found heart breaking conditions at this orphanage.*

Six of us were in the air conditioned cab and eight people were in the back of the truck. I sat in the back seat behind Craig who was driving and Pastor John and Ariel and Macrae sat in the front seat. Michelle and Randy rode in the back seat with me. The trade off was that we had the air-conditioning, but the people riding in the bed of the truck had a much better feel of Haiti, with views of the mountains and the incredible rubble and the sights and sounds of the people in the streets. Of course, this was accompanied by a much rougher ride.

Peter (right) & Rodney in the back of the truck.

Some of the people riding in the back were standing up. Peter was in the back. I abandoned the thought of all the safety violations, conscious of the vehicle hitting all of those pot holes, with people in the bed of the truck bouncing around. I decided to trust the Lord and enjoy the adventure, instead of fretting over something I couldn't change.

Haitians- A Beautiful People

We wound through the streets of Haiti. People were displaying their goods to sell: chickens, clothes, fruit, paintings, anything you could think of and more! I craned my neck to see through the window trying not to appear to be staring.

Haitians are a beautiful people! They have beautiful features and are very attractive. For the most part, they dress nicely as well. Their clothes look good and seem well fitting and many of them dress up with heels and the like. There are times you see people who are dirty or don't have shoes, but that is what you might expect from such living conditions.

The people at the church services are especially nicely dressed. Their clothes are crisp and clean, and the women fix their hair with brightly colored barrettes and headbands. The men wear long sleeve shirts and some suits. The people take very good care of the clothes that they have.

They live in searing heat in tents or small shanties with no air-conditioning, no showers with clean water, no washer and dryers! Amazing! It seems so incongruent, it almost makes your head spin. How on earth do they do it?

Haitians are a friendly people, too. When our eyes would meet from our vehicle many would smile and wave. But not everyone, a few of the people were not happy to see us, one man scowled at us as we drove by. Then, he threw up his middle finger with a wild gesture, making sure we would notice. But the majority of Haitians seemed to really appreciate people who came to help.

My swim instructor, who had been to Haiti before our trip, told me that some of the people would not be happy to have us in their country. "Don't take it personally," she said. "They have been through a lot."

After a long ride, we came upon a cobblestone hill. Craig stopped the truck and jumped out. He went to the back of the truck and told everyone in the back to hang on. I wondered what was going on as I peered at the steep street looming in front of us. He jumped back into his seat, slammed down on the gas pedal with great force and the truck took a gulp and lurched forward in a burst of power.

My swim instructor told me that some people would not be happy to have us in their country. "Don't take it personally,". she said. "They have been through a lot."

I looked back to see if everyone was still inside the bed of the truck, but I couldn't tell. The people standing up were blocking the view of the others. The truck came to a grinding halt at the top of the hill. We had arrived at the orphanage.

We were now in the mountains. The hills were covered with green foliage and dotted with small houses. It was refreshing, because it was cooler than in Port-au-Prince by ten degrees, which made it nice.

The orphanage was a three story building with a big red gate, that was attached to a wall..with razor wire...but this razor wire was being used as a clothes line!

The orphanage was a three story building with a big red gate in front of it that was attached to a wall with the familiar circles of razor wire atop it, but this razor wire had clothes hanging from it! It was being used as a clothes line!

Craig and Paul pushed back the gate so that we could drive in. "Everyone out, I need to get a good run at this hill," Craig boomed. Looking up at the steep driveway I understood why. We poured out of the vehicle and stood on the street watching as Craig barreled up the driveway and then jolted to a stop. Afterward we went in, they pushed the gate back shut. Gates are very important for safety in Haiti. Earlier someone had come to the orphanage and tried to take a couple of the children saying that they were "their" children. The intruders made the mistake of pointing to the pastor's biological son when claiming who "their" children were. The caregiver did not open the gate to them.

When we opened the front door to go inside, we were greeted by a staircase. We went single file up the three flights of stairs and stepped out into a small kitchen that was painted a happy bright yellow.

Gates are very important for safety in Haiti. Earlier someone had come to the orphanage and tried to take a couple of the children...

Two Haitian women were working in the kitchen. An older lady with her hair pulled back was standing at the stove cooking. She began briskly stirring a pot of something that was bubbling on top of the stove. She looked over at me and flashed a sweet smile. Her face was full of kindness and gentleness. The young

Haitian woman washing dishes at the sink glanced over her shoulder, brushing back one of her braids. Her young face looked haggard.

Pastor Bellande, the Haitian pastor who runs the orphanage, appeared from a doorway looking smart in a white short sleeved shirt and crisp black pants. He greeted us warmly. "Hello!" he said. "Thank you all so much for coming!"

The Children

The children all crowded around our group as we squeezed into the kitchen and overflowed into the dining/family room. You could tell that they were very excited to see us, but still a bit apprehensive. The surgical scrubs that I had found at Goodwill were just right for the occasion. My pants were bright purple and the top I had on was a mixture of pale and bright purple. It had two big pockets on the front and the material had tons of big jolly brown teddy bears. It was way too big for me which made me look three or four sizes bigger than I really am, but when I tried it on in the store and looked in the mirror all I could think of was how happy the little children would feel staring into the faces of all those smiling teddy bears.

I reached into one of my large pockets where I had hidden handfuls of bright stickers and a few pieces of candy. I stuck out my hand and gave the first little boy I saw a sticker and then I pulled out another sticker for a young girl who was standing by the stove. They smiled back at me and took the stickers, but I could tell that they weren't quite sure what to do with them.

They smiled back at me, and took the stickers but I could tell that they weren't quite sure what to do with them.

"Maybe they have never seen a sticker," I thought. I bent down and peeled the sticker off of the paper and put it on the back of the little boy's hand. He looked up at me and smiled, his big brown eyes glowing. Some language is universal and joy is spoken in every language.

Craig picked up a small girl who was standing by the stove. She was dressed very cheery wearing a white short-sleeved shirt with small purple and pink fish on it. She had bright barrettes holding back her braided hair, but the saddest eyes I have ever experienced peered out from her little face.

Craig held her out and tried to get her to come to me. She looked back at him and then to me and then reluctantly let me hold her. The sadness pooled in her eyes and emanated from her face. She squeezed me tightly. She just wanted to be held, to feel love. She was the newest addition to the house and by far the saddest.

It was a hard fact to swallow, that all nine of these children's parents were dead.

After awhile, Michelle asked me if she could hold her. The little girl sat on her lap and snuggled close to her.

It was a hard fact to swallow that all nine of these children's parents were dead. Michelle locked eyes with Peter, and they both got tears in their eyes, overcome with the emotion of it all.

I looked around and everyone in our group was interacting with the children.

Chuck was playing boo with a little guy with long curly eyelashes and a huge smile who was giggling loudly.

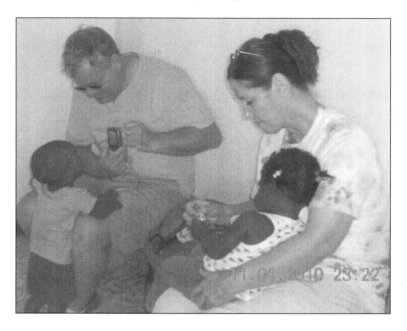

Peter showing a child my pink camera. Michelle cuddles a child.

Peter was in the corner conversing with a child who was wide-eyed with fascination over his picture on my hot pink camera screen.

Paul was holding a very thin little girl with tight curly hair, who had wrapped her arms around his neck and was squeezing him.

Pastor John was on the balcony lifting a tiny girl in a bright orange dress up and down. She was making joyful, happy sounds every time she went into the air.

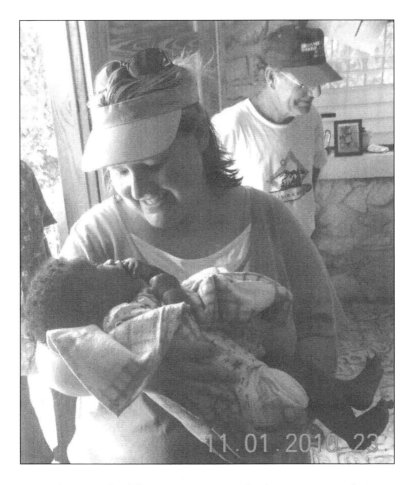

Charity held a miniature baby wrapped in a blanket in her arms. They gazed tenderly at one another. The baby's eyes were so big they seemed to swallow her entire face.

Macrae was holding hands with a wispy child, they were dancing to imaginary music. They swayed back and forth and then spun in wide circles.

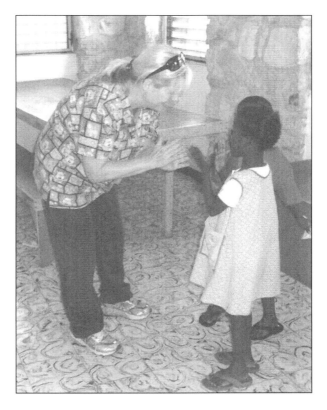

Me, playing "Patty Cake"

Everyone was interacting with these magnetic Haitian children. I looked around and realized that all of these little children were well-dressed and clean and healthy and loved.

I felt so thankful for this place and Pastor Bellande and his wife. Pastor Bellande was making a big difference in their lives.

Pastor Bellande had plans to take in twenty chil-

> "How did you decide to take in all of these children?" I inquired. "I was an orphan myself," he began, "So I know how it feels...

dren when he was equipped to do so. He wanted to do it right, to be sure the children always had everything that they needed first.

From what I could tell, the children ranged in age from a ten months old to ten years old. I wandered outside on the balcony to talk to Pastor Bellande. Peter and Pastor John were out there too. I began to ask this gentle man who was brimming with the presence of God, some of the questions that were racing through my head. "How did you decide to take in all of these children?" I inquired.

An Extraordinary Man Takes The Challenge

"I was an orphan myself," he began, "So I know how it feels to not have any parents. After the terrible earthquake, I decided to take children into my home. We opened the home in May."

"Is it a challenge?" I asked, thinking of the tiny boy full of life and youthful energy I had seen earlier going around and around in circles on the floor.

"Yes!" he said. "Some days are more challenging than others, but every day is a challenge. But, it will be worth everything if I can save just one of them," he said with resolve.

"Is it a challenge?" I asked, thinking of the tiny boy full of youthful energy...going around and around in circles on the floor.

I asked him what he needed for help to run the orphanage. "I work full-time, and my wife works full-time," he explained. "We need caregivers for the children. We need money for the tuition to send the kids to school. The kids must wear uniforms to school, and they need lunches every day, so we need funds for that as well. We also need food to feed the children every day. There are many expenses to properly taking care of our children," he said.

I thought of the mountain of laundry that they must have to wash by hand in the streams every day and hang up to dry and the patience and love you would have to possess to help all of these children.

"Will these children ever be able to be adopted?" I asked. I glanced at a child sitting quietly in Elder's lap. He was examining Elder's floppy hat.

"No, I don't think so," Pastor Bellande continued, "The Haitian government requires a lot of paperwork for

"Will these children ever be able to be adopted?" I asked. "No, I don't think so,...thousands (of parents) are still missing and buried under the rubble, ...many records are destroyed."

an adoption to occur. If the parents are alive and want a child to live in an orphanage because they cannot care for them, both parents must sign papers to relinquish their rights.

But in this case, the parents are dead. The government requires proof that both parents are dead. This is almost impossible to prove. There are still hundreds of thousands of people missing and buried under earthquake rubble. Many of the records that could prove that people are dead were destroyed in the earthquake."

Even though this was the case, Pastor Bellande was prepared to raise all of these children until they were adults.

I asked him more about the earthquake, and he continued with an incredible story. "I thought I was going to die when everything started shaking. I held up my hands, and I could not move. The only thing I could say was 'Jesus! Jesus! Jesus!' as I saw the building crumbling all around me. Then it stopped, and I was still here.

> "I thought I was going to die when everything started shaking. I held up my hands and could not move."

My mother-in-law, who is a good woman, was buried under the rubble. We dug her out from underneath the rubble, and she only had cuts and scrapes. No one in my family or my church died. It was amazing," he said with joy.

After a while we went to the truck to retrieve the backpacks that we had filled with toys that our group had brought from America just for them.

The backpacks were all different colors, and we had them filled to overflowing with soft beanie babies to squeeze and plastic children's instruments like harmonicas and tambourines to make music.

The backpacks were all different colors, and ...overflowing with... wonderful toys that we knew these kids would love.

There were jump ropes to toss and toy cars to run over floors and stuffed animals to hug and all kinds of wonderful toys that we knew these kids would love.

We even brought brightly colored kites that they could run through the house and let trail behind them or take outside and experience them sailing high in the sky in the wind over the beautiful green hills.

We had been told before our trip how expensive toilet paper was so we purposely tucked a soft white roll into each backpack.

We all moved to the dining/family room because it was larger than the small kitchen to open the backpacks.

This room was shaped like a rectangle and had a big arching window surrounded by stone on one end. In front of the window was a long wooden table with benches on either side for dining. I could almost imagine the children sitting at the table, side-by-side on the benches, chattering away and enjoying their meals in that happy arrangement.

The other wall had a row of jalousie windows, often referred to as louvered windows. They are like shutters made of glass that you can open and close. These kinds of windows are extremely popular in tropical climates and are often used in porches and breezeways that are not air conditioned because they allow the cool breezes indoors while still being able to shield from the rain and other elements.

Underneath one of the jalousie windows was a small wooden bench that was also used as a toy box. Next to the jalousie windows was a sliding glass door. It was open, and it exposed an attached balcony.

The long balcony outside was surrounded by a wrought iron fence so the kids could go outside and enjoy the view of a large pond across the street, the mountains and the fresh air.

The home actually had two balconies, the other was just below this one on the second floor, but this one was the largest.

Inside the room the floor had a brown and white swirl patterned ceramic tile and the only furniture besides the table and toy box bench were wooden benches that lined the sides of the walls.

This place was nothing like the horrible orphanages that I had read about online. It was a nice, clean place, filled with love.

Almost Christmas Morning

The atmosphere was electric when we brought in the backpacks. The children all crowded around to see what we had brought. Opening the backpacks was like the exciting confusion of Christmas morning when everyone is tearing into wrapping paper opening their presents. We gave each child a backpack, and then helped them unzip them. They began pulling out strange American toys, some of which they had never seen. The glee on their little faces was incredible. It felt wonderful to be able to give a small bit of joy to these little people who had lost so much.

There were smiles all around as the children tried to figure out how to play with these unfamiliar American toys.

"This is how you blow on a harmonica," I said opening the package and blowing on it for one little boy with huge brown eyes. In a flash, he grabbed it from my hand and began blowing on it, making little bursts of sound.

Trying to show a little girl how to use a jump rope that had candy-filled ends, I tripped on the rope with my big clunky tennis shoes. The end of it crashed to the floor and the candy inside spilled out. The little girl rushed to grab the three pink balls that went rolling out across the floor. She quickly retrieved them and popped them into her mouth. I had broken the end of the jump rope. It was still useable, but I felt bad.

Chapter Ten: The Orphanage
Study It!

1. Read 1 John 3:16. Why does making a difference sometimes mean sacrificing?

2. Pastor Bellande, talking about the orphans said, "Some days are more challenging than others, but every day is a challenge. But it will be worth everything if I can save just one of them." Why is it important to do what you can do, even against big odds?

3. What does it mean when the author says, "You will make a difference for the glory of God, even though you may never know what that difference was?"

4. Can you think of a way that you can make a positive difference in the life of one person today? What is it?

Chapter 11

Connections

On your God-designed adventure you could be sent to a place where you may meet people and see places where practically all of the world's trappings of wealth are torn away or missing. In the human body, when one sense is taken away your other senses will be stronger to compensate for the lack. For example, a person who cannot see sometimes hears very keenly. At times, when people have very few physical belongings and comforts, they are more in touch with the spiritual side of things. Observe how the people you meet in these conditions connect with the spiritual world. You will be amazed!

Soon it was time to leave the orphanage. We said our good-byes and piled back into the truck. Outside of the orphanage were five little neighbor boys. They ran to our truck in happy anticipation. I had a few stickers left, and I peeled off a fish and stuck it on the hand of one of the little boys. He looked like he was about eight years old. He smiled as he looked down at his hand. His older brother wanted a sticker, too. I peeled another one off, this time a purple starfish. He took it and put it on his forehead and looked at himself in the side mirror of the truck.

The little boys wanted their picture taken. "Photo, photo," they said. We clicked some pictures posing with them, and of course, they wanted to see each one on the digital screen. Picture taking can be a sticky subject in Haiti. Many times the older people do not want their pictures taken, but the children love it. They are always begging, "Photo! Photo!"

As we drove away we could hear the exuberant noise of the orphanage children on the balcony playing with their new toys.

Before long we were stopping at a point where some of the Haitian people had little areas set up to sell their wares: paintings, sculptures, little mahogany boxes, and jewelry.

The view on this point was incredible! Below, dotting the hillside, were little white tents packed together and leaning against one another. There were so many tents I couldn't even count them! Could this be one of the tent cities I had heard so much about?

There were so many tents I couldn't even count them. Could this be one of the tent cities I had heard so much about?

Farther beyond them in the distance, was a beautiful blue sea and buildings of all kinds. "Is that the Presidential Palace?" Randy asked pointing to one of the buildings below. Paul surveyed the situation. "No, I think it may be over there," he said, pointing in another direction. Everyone was chattering away, drinking in the magnificent view. Camera's came out of pockets and people began snapping pictures to capture the magic for their loved ones at home.

It was all quite inviting to view, but more interesting to me than the breathtaking view or anything in it was the thin man with a white shirt standing ten feet away from the group.

He caught my eye and something about him drew me to him. I walked up to him, glancing at the paintings he had for sale.

"See this one?" he said pointing to a large painting with huge sailboats floating on a sea of turquoise blue water. "I will give it to you for four hundred dollars."

"It is beautiful," I said admiring the painting, "but I cannot give you four hundred dollars for it." I paused, "Instead, I will pray for you. What is your request?" I asked.

...but more interesting to me than the breathtaking view or anything in it, was the thin man with a white shirt standing ten feet away from the group...something about him drew me to him.

He looked pensive, but not surprised that I had asked to pray for him.

"I am sad. I hurt for my people. Pray for Haiti," he said.

"You are sad?" I repeated.

"Yes," he said. "I need safety. It is dangerous here. I am afraid that someone will rob me. Pray for me because sometimes I am sick and cannot work." I looked into his eyes and felt overwhelmed with God's love for him. I knew God had seen his plight.

"Thank you for the prayers! They are more important to me than money."

"God sent me from America to pray for you," I said, "and he will do miracles on your behalf!"

I asked him his name, and after a couple of failed attempts at pronouncing it, he told me to call him Junior. God knows his name. God knew his situation. He sees each one of us. When I finished praying for him, he was very appreciative.

"Thank you for the prayers! They are more important to me than money." In a country where survival is an everyday struggle I knew that meant a lot.

Then he said it, "Jesus is my life." His words hit me with powerful force. I had never heard anyone describe their relationship with Jesus like that. The words and their impacted swept over me and settled deep within me. Not just a part, but my very survival, my everything! I could not exist without Him. It is

Then he said it, "Jesus is my life." His words hit me with powerful force...settled deep within me.

right on target with the Bible and what God wants for each of us.

"You have said, Seek My face (inquire for and require My presence as your vital need), My heart says to You, Your face (Your presence) Lord, will I seek, inquire for, and require (of necessity and on the authority of Your Word)."

-Psalms 27:8 (AMP)

When all of the trappings of material wealth are pulled away, sometimes people see Jesus more clearly. They depend on Him for everything. Yet in a country where are all our needs are more easily met, it is easy to make Jesus only a part of our lives.

I purchased a statue of a woman holding a baby from another vendor. We finally got back into the truck, amidst a crowd of vendors vying for our attention.

"Please, buy this! I need the money!" an older man shouted at me through the closed truck window holding up two small statues. One of the statues slipped out of his hand, and broke on the ground. I was afraid he would be angry, but he ran away and was back at the window with another statue that looked just the same.

> *I felt determined to remember this man in my prayers. I can still see his face, I can still feel his pain.*

If Peter had not been in the back of the truck with all of our money, I would have purchased the statues.

I noticed the thin man in the white shirt had come to the truck from his position on the overlook to stand and watch me. He waved. His eyes said thank you. He watched intently as we drove out of sight. I felt determined to remember this man in my prayers. I can still see his face; I can still

... feel his pain.

Unforgettable, he is still in my prayers.

Chapter Eleven: Connections
Study It!

1. Junior says, "Jesus is my life!" What do you think that means? How can you make Jesus your life?

2. Why do you think that people with very few material goods sometimes see Jesus more clearly?

3. Find Psalms 27:8 in this chapter. Read it. How would it change your life to require Christ as your vital need?

4. Junior tells Jan that her prayers were more important than money. What do you think he meant by that?

5. If your prayers are more important than money, who will you choose to pray for today? Write down their name _____ . Now, say a prayer for them.

Chapter 12

PROVISION

Sometimes, we think we are in charge of our own destiny, our own provision, but when it comes right down to it, everything we have is provided by God. It is easy to be like Moses, when God asked him to speak for Him he replied,

"O my Lord, I have never been eloquent, neither in the past, nor since you have spoken to your servant. I am slow of speech and tongue."

"Who gave man his mouth? Who makes him deaf or mute? Who gives him sight or makes him blind? Is it not I, the Lord?"

-EX 4: 10, 11 (NIV)

Trust God to come through for you with whatever you need, in every situation. He will never let you down. When you plan to ride a bus, when do you give the bus driver your ticket? It is when you enter the bus and not before. In the same way grace will be given to you, just when you need it. Don't sweat it, or stress, just count on it to be there, waiting for you.

We saw the incredible destruction of the earthquake on this trip as we drove through the dusty winding streets. We could understand why so many people had died and were still buried in the rubble. All of the buildings were made of heavy concrete block and were not reinforced. When they fell, it was with terrible force. The rubble was everywhere, crumbling pillars, caved in roofs, complete decimation.

Most of the equipment that they have to clear the rubble away, if they have any at all, is just a wheelbarrow and shovels. Most of the rubble must be carried away by hand. Even when this is done, where do you put the tremendous volume of debris? There is no good place. We didn't see even one piece of heavy equipment on our trip. But we did see many people trying to clean it up, even though the progress seemed very slow. Three men were standing on the roof of a crumbled building. One of them balanced a wheel barrow, while the others were trying to fill it. Here and there, we saw people were trying to get rid of the mess and find their buried loved ones.

Still, even with all of the terrible destruction, there were many stories of how God had miraculously worked to help people.

Still, even with all of the terrible destruction, there were many stories of how God had miraculously worked....

Sometimes, He changed situations like the pastor who was supposed to be at an internet café when the earthquake hit. Everyone there had died in the quake, but he had not made it that day as was his usual habit. His car had not started that morning, and he was late.

The incredible story of the new truck that the missionary had just been given that was parked right next to a building and during the quake bounced into the middle of the street escaping the building that fell into its former parking spot. The Voodoo priest who called out to Jesus when things began shaking, because he knew that was where the real help would come. I knew there were many stories that I had not yet heard, stories of God's miraculous provision in the midst of horrible chaos.

Riding in the back of the truck, Peter & Rodney view the destruction.

English Class

When we arrived back at the base, it was time for the English class. John and Debbie were the base camp leaders. They had pastored a church in Arizona and now had felt called to come to Haiti. They had been in Haiti for eight months with a two year commitment. Debbie, a former teacher, had set up the program to teach English in March, and I was amazed at how much English the people knew already. She is a beautiful woman who is stylish in the midst of incredible heat and tough conditions. I marveled at how she stayed so pristine in this place. Rachel, the young girl who helps, is just the same. I could not figure out how they did it. The second day I gave up on my make-up and I took on the "missionary look" that these glamorous woman did not portray.

How Many Coconuts Can You Put In An Empty Sack?

After a lesson from Debbie with the whole group, we broke into smaller groups and taught the Haitians the meaning of American proverbs and then asked them the meaning of Haitian proverbs. The Haitian people love proverbs, storytelling and riddles. Riddles are a form of humor. "How many coconuts can you put into an empty sack? Answer: Only one. After that the sack is not empty." One of the Haitian proverbs was "Money makes the dog dance." "What does that mean?" I asked the small group of Haitians that sat in a little circle on metal chairs with Michelle and me.

"It means that money can make a lot happen for you!" one of the young men offered. After he gave his answer, he stood up and did a little dance, turning in a circle, then sat down with a smile. We all laughed. Listening to them explain Haitian proverbs was really fun.

Connecting with the people was one of the best parts of this trip. I loved the Haitian people!

> After the meeting, a young man gave me his e-mail address. "You will not forget me?" he pleaded.

After the meeting, a young man who was in our small group gave me his e-mail address. "You will not forget me?" he pleaded. I was so happy for the opportunities that we were given by the base camp leaders to allow us to connect with the people.

Later that night it was pouring rain. The base leaders decided to give us a treat and take our team out to a local restaurant for some Haitian food.

Craig asked for our orders so that he could call them into the restaurant before we left so the dinners would be ready when we arrived. We asked for his recommendations. "You have three choices," he said. "They are goat, which is usually very dry and really fatty, barbeque chicken, which is not the American barbeque sauce you are used to and chicken with sauce. I like everything, but I think that my favorite is the chicken with sauce," he grinned. Most of us ordered that.

At an intersection a car was approaching us head on. "Oh he'll move,"...I was not so sure.

Peter and I and Pastor John rode with Debbie, the base camp leader's wife. As she pulled out, I asked her how often she had driven in Haiti, thinking of the crazy traffic and drivers. "I don't get the chance to drive here very often," she said. The rain was pouring down in sheets as she drove through the muddy streets. We bounced as she hit potholes and swerved to avoid others. At an intersection a car was approaching us head on. "Oh he'll move," Debbie said nonchalantly; I was not so sure. I braced myself, trying not to tense up. At the last minute, she slammed on the brakes and let the driver pass. I couldn't wait to get to the restaurant. I was thankful that she was driving and not me. We pulled into a driveway right in front of the restaurant and got out.

There were two men with shotguns standing outside in the pouring rain guarding the restaurant. I understood why they had to call ahead to order. I thought to myself how strange it was to have to hire gunmen, just to allow people to be safe enough to go out to eat.

How strange it was to have to hire gunmen, just to allow people to be safe enough..to go out to eat.

We sat at a long table with a white linen tablecloth. There were soft glowing candles on each table. The dimly lit place had a flat screen TV just above our table. The screen, which was mostly static with an occasional picture that looked like a government station, jumped in and out of focus. I wondered why they even bothered to have a TV at all. This had to be a luxury of the rich only, but who would want to watch it?

When the meal arrived in the dark light, I couldn't really tell what it was. The food was covered in an orange sauce. I poked the chicken with my fork. It was hard as a rock. "Oh, my goodness, what kind of chicken is this going to be?" I inwardly gasped. I poked my fork into the other blob on the plate, and it sunk in. I soon discovered that the second pile was the chicken and the other pile covered in sauce was a fried plantain (banana). They brought out two kinds of rice near the end of the meal, one I liked and the other, not so much.

Peter and I each had a bottle of soda with our meal. They serve soda in glass bottles like America did in the sixties.

I really liked most of the Haitian food. Sometimes the appearance of it wasn't so good, but the taste was what really counted! I sat at the very end of the table and enjoyed the conversation with Peter and Randy.

The rain had mostly stopped when we left. We ran between the droplets and jumped back into our waiting truck guarded by gunmen. Soon, we were back at the base camp.

Chapter Twelve: Provision
Study It!

1. Have you ever felt inadequate to do something you knew God wanted you to do? Describe the situation.

2. Has God ever provided for you when you had a great need? What happened?

3. Why do people think that they are in charge of their own provision?

4. Is there something that God wants you to do today that you cannot do in your own strength? Write it down and then read Philippians 4:13.

Chapter 13

Divine Appointments

No matter who you are, or where you are, God has already set up appointments for you. He has written them neatly in His book with your name on them. They are divine appointments. If you decide to take these appointments, you will find that God has placed them in His timeline just for you, to bring Him glory. They may be with people that you have already planned to meet or more than likely, they will be surprises. They will be with folks that you never expected to find, individuals that you will treasure. Their faces, which you will not soon forget, will be etched into your heart. And their lives will impact your life forever!

When we woke up in the morning, we had no idea that this would be our last full day in Haiti.

The plan was again for the men to build a home for one of the church members who had been living in a tent. It was not to be. The woman had decided she did not want to take her tent down and risk having no where to stay in the hurricane.

We were told we would help with projects at the church a block away. We could varnish benches, cut out more benches and work on making pavers for the people to sell.

Michelle, Charity and I settled down painting varnish on the benches. The benches would be used in the school. Peter, Randy, Pastor John and Elder were helping with the pavers. They were mixing rocks to make cement and then pouring the cement into little octagon wooden frames to make pavers for the church to sell. They were experimenting with projects, so that the church people could become self supporting. Pavers seemed like a good idea, as they were easy to make and fulfilled a need.

Paul took Macrae, Ariel and Frank to cut out more benches. Macrae and Ariel knew how to work with wood and saws, since their grandfather had been in construction. He made sure they had those skills too. Rodney was back at the house fixing something.

Painting the varnish was a sticky mess. We had thin plastic gloves that stuck to the paint brushes. The first container of varnish I began using was too thick. We were told to use all that we could since materials were often scare.

On the first bench, I soon discovered that using

this container was not going to work. The varnish puddled and oozed on the bench in great sticky gobs. I began sharing Charity's varnish can. We worked until lunch finishing four sets of benches.

An Appointment With A Hurricane?

Then we headed back for the traditional sandwiches of ham, salami, and cheese with the usual side of fruit. Unlike the Haitians, we had the luxury of three meals, just like in America. We gathered outside in the backyard and sat around a long wooden table. Pastor John cleared his throat. "I have an announcement to make he said. "We need to leave Haiti tomorrow. I know you have counted on being here for two more days, but Hurricane Tomas is headed right towards Port-au-Prince and will be here soon. American Airlines wants to evacuate us right away. Kathy talked to them this morning. She has all the flights set up for tomorrow morning." Kathy, Pastor John's wife, was our contact in America.

Hurricane Tomas is headed right towards Port-au-Prince and will be here soon.

After lunch we were supposed to go back and finish the work we had started that morning. We also had plans to go to the tent city in the afternoon and do the gospel presentation that I had put together in Tulsa. I was really excited about doing the gospel presentation. We would finally get the chance and just before we had to leave.

After lunch, I felt compelled to stay behind. I didn't want the others to think I was lazy, but somehow I felt God wanted me there. I would pray for the gospel presentation and have it ready.

In anticipation of our departure the next day, I began to unpack the food that I had brought from my suitcase that was unused. Boy, did I ever bring too much food! I went downstairs with it and saw a Haitian man busy with his laptop sitting in the living room at a small card table. I pulled a few things out of the bag and politely interrupted him. "Would you like some food?" I asked. He stopped and looked up. His face said it all. This was important to him.

God Planned Stuff, Under The Table

"Oh, thank you," he said. "May God bless you!" Encouraged, I began to unload most of it. And then I looked under the table and pulled out a bag my mother had sent for someone in Haiti. Somehow, it had missed the stockpiling in the garage. I opened the bag to find a set of razors, a sewing kit, toothbrushes, toothpaste, and all kinds of things! I was amazed at his joy over the simple things. A few bars of soap were like gold, and the cheap plastic watch that was included in the bag was an obvious hit.

I remembered when my mom bought all the supplies I was doubtful." Do you think that people will really want all of this stuff?" I asked her.

"Oh, a watch! I really have needed a watch," he said. I remembered when my mom bought all the supplies. I had been doubtful.

"Do you think that people will really want all of this stuff?" I asked her. I was thinking about how much my suitcase held, and I was doubtful it would all fit.

"Oh, yes!" she exclaimed. She had painstakingly thought out each purchase: antibiotic ointment, a pair of reading glasses, all kinds of things.

Apparently, God had directed my mom to get these items especially for this dear man. His pack was completely full when I was done!

Then he told me his story. His name was Pastor Fredrick. He was interpreting an English document into French for the base camp so that he could earn some money. The story began with him being able to go to America.

He loved America and all of its comforts. He was eager to stay there. Another pastor was going to help him stay in America by setting up a meeting with an American congressman. The plan was set for him to talk to the congressman and get permission to stay on longer. "It is very likely that your request will be granted to stay in America my friend," the pastor told him. "I know this congressman and he is very kind. I will go with you to talk to him"

"It is very likely that your request will be granted to stay in America my friend," the pastor told him.

"Even though I wanted to stay in America with

all my heart," he exclaimed, "I began to feel like God was calling me to go back to Haiti. I did not want to go. I decided to ask God for a sign to prove to me that I should go back to Haiti. I tried to make it hard for God because I did NOT want to go back to Haiti. 'Please God,' I prayed. 'If you want me to go back to Haiti, have someone call me very early in the morning and tell me that I need to go to back to Haiti.' Wouldn't you know it? The very next morning at 6 a.m. my phone was ringing. When I answered it, it was a pastor friend of mine that I had not talked to in awhile. He told me that he thought that God wanted me to go back to Haiti. He told me, 'Do not stay in America. God wants you in Haiti.'"

Pastor Fredrick paused reflecting back to his hard decision, "I was still not convinced when I hung up, because I really, really did not want to go back to Haiti.

'Okay God' I said, 'I need another sign. Have someone else tell me today before I go to meet with the American congressman that I should go back to Haiti.' Right before my friend was to come to pick me up to talk to the American congressman, there was a knock at my door. When I opened the door,

"I slept in an abandoned school with no electric, no water for the first three months. Next, I lived for two months in an earthquake destroyed house."

there stood another friend of mine. 'I am sorry to bother you,' my friend said, 'but I felt compelled to come over here and tell you that I really think God wants you to go back to Haiti and not stay in America.'

After my friend left, I looked at the time. Any minute the pastor was going to pick me up to talk to the congressman. 'Okay God,' I said 'I will go back to Haiti.' I picked up the phone and called my friend. 'Do not pick me up; I am going back to Haiti. God wants me to do it.'

I slept in an abandoned school with no electric and no water for the first three months. Next I lived for two months in an earthquake-destroyed house with my brother. We lived in two rooms and had no water and no electric." I don't know where he is staying now.

"Have you seen what voodoo does to people?"

he asked me with a faraway look.

"No," I said.

"It is terrible," he paused, scrunching his face as if playing out a gruesome scene in his mind. "The torture of women, of the children, is awful." He paused again. I could see the pain in his eyes. "They need help," he continued. "They need Jesus. I have to tell them about Jesus so they can be free," he said.

Suddenly, I felt very small, like I was in the presence of a president or a king of some kind. This man had given up everything to follow Jesus.

Suddenly, I felt very small, like I was in the presence of a president or a king of some kind. This man had given up everything to follow Jesus. I had struggled to go on a small mission trip for a very short time. The theme was pervasive. "Jesus is my life!"

Craig came back and told me that no one wanted to go to the tent camp to minister; they wanted to continue working on the various projects at the church. "Everyone?" I questioned, "Did you ask Pastor John?"

"No," he said.

"Please, ask Pastor John," I pleaded.

George had told me, "You might have opposition trying to share this gospel presentation, but don't give up, just pray. God will open the doors so you can share it."

"You might have opposition trying to share this gospel presentation, but don't give up, just pray. God will open the doors so you can share it."

When Craig left, I prayed, "This is Your message; please make a way for it."

I was also wrestling with what to do with the CD player, the shirts, and the gospel presentation in Creole that we had brought for the people. I had thought earlier that I should give it to Geraldo, a 16-year-old Haitian kid who had told me that his mission was to spread the gospel. He said he would take good care of it and have people listen to it. He would have a party and invite people to come and listen to the message. When I talked to the director, she said I could leave it with them and the church could check it out to people. I was conflicted about what to do. "God," I prayed, "If you want Geraldo to have this gospel presentation to use, please let him be at the camp tonight when we go to share the presentation."

I talked to Rachel and helped her with some art ideas that she planned to do with the English class. Then I sat down in the living room and prayed and read the Bible. I came across some verses that really stuck out to me in the book of Joshua.

Be strong and of a good courage; for unto this people shalt though divide for an inheritance the land, which I swore unto their fathers to give them.

Have not I commanded thee? Be strong and of a good courage; be not afraid, neither be thou dismayed: for the LORD thy God (is) with thee whithersoever thou goest.

The Lord your God hath given you rest and hath given you this land.

-Joshua 1:6, 9 and last half of 13 (KJV)

These verses jumped from the page straight to

my heart. Peter came in and I read them to him, then to Rodney.

Later, as Pastor Fredrick started to leave, I got up to tell him good-bye. I started to talk to him, but was interrupted by his phone ringing. I sat down.

"You have a word from the Lord for me." It was not a question, but a statement... the words sprung from my lips...

In a minute, he clicked off his phone and came over. "You have a word from the Lord for me." It was not a question, it was a statement. The words sprung from my lips, the Holy Spirit bringing them like a fountain.

"God is going to use you to restore Haiti!" And then I read him the verses in Joshua that had stood out to me, but didn't quite seem to be for me. "As God has filled your empty backpack today," I told him, "God will fill you with the things that you need by His grace." The words and the message bubbled up in me supernaturally.

When I was finished he said, "Amazing! Four different people from four different countries have told me the very same thing! They have all said that God would use me to restore Haiti! Two weeks ago a pastor's wife told me the very same things you just told me, even to the exact verses from Joshua that you just shared."

"Really?" I was thrilled! God had lined this meeting up perfectly.

Gods Makes A Way

Suddenly Craig burst in the door, "Are you ready to go?"

"Of course!" I said. I grabbed the bag full of supplies and rushed out the door. When we pulled into the camp, the sun was sinking slowly in the sky, we did not have an abundance of daylight left. Two men were welding something with a generator making a loud roar.

"We have to set up somewhere else," Craig said. We got back into the truck and went a little deeper into the camp. We piled out of the truck and there was Geraldo.

"Mama, Mama," he cried, "I came!" I felt so

much joy. I knew God wanted this sixteen- year- old boy to have this gospel presentation.

I hugged him tightly and told him, "I am so glad!" Getting down to business we passed out the tee shirts for our presentation. Elder was not there. "Who is going to wear the white shirt?" I questioned. Peter pointed to a man from Hawaii who had just come to the base camp and had piled into the truck with us.

"He can wear it," Peter said.

"Mama, Mama," he cried, "I came!"...I knew God wanted this sixteen year old to have this presentation.

"But, he doesn't even know what we are doing," I replied, panicked, ignoring the fact that the guy was standing right beside me. He had never seen the presentation.

"Do you want to help us by wearing this shirt?" Peter asked him. He nodded a cheerful yes. I handed him the shirt and briefly told him what he was suppose to do. He graciously complied.

There was no time for long explanations. Earlier, Craig had told us he did not know if anyone would show up for us to do the gospel presentation, but they were showing up in droves.

I motioned to some men who were walking down the dirt road. There were children outside playing and mothers milling about. I waved for them to come too. How many people were there?

Then I asked Geraldo to tell the people to draw near and he too motioned to them calling out loudly in Creole, bidding them to come.

"We can't wait any longer! Start this!" Craig said. "Geraldo, tell the people to get quiet," he said. They responded. A silence settled over the crowd and with a push of a button George was talking to them. They listened. We did actions with the different colored shirts. Each one of us with the different colored shirt performed our meager action as the crowd watched intently.

I raised my arms to the sky and smiled, wearing the bright yellow shirt that represented heaven. In Creole George told the people about heaven and the streets made of pure gold. He told them there would be no more sorrow or pain. He told them there would be no more earthquakes in heaven. "God is there and it is wonderful", he explained.

> *He told them there would be no more earthquakes in heaven. "God is there and it is wonderful"...*

Then Pastor John wearing the black shirt bowed his head in shame. George shared that sin is what keeps us from heaven. Sin is anything that is disobedience to God and the fact that we are all sinners.

Michelle stepped up with her red t-shirt and stretched her arms out like a cross and bowed her head. George began to explain how Jesus shed his blood and took the punishment for our sins. He made a bridge for us to God by dying on the cross. He died on the cross and rose again on the third day.

The man in the white shirt who was thrown into his duty began to rub where his heart was as George told the crowd that the blood of Jesus would wash their hearts clean by his blood. "He will wash away every bad thing you have done. He will forgive you and live in your heart."

Then George told the people how they could go to heaven, how they could know God.

"Pray with me," he asked the people in perfect Creole,

Here, in this foreign land as darkness was falling people were lifting their voices in unison, praying in their own language, out loud with George!

"Dear Jesus, I believe that you died on the cross to take the punishment for my sins and became alive again. Please forgive me of my sins and make me new inside, like you promised. I confess you as my Lord and Savior. Thank you for making a place in heaven for me. Amen."

This Is Why We Came To Haiti

Here, in this foreign land as darkness was falling people were lifting their voices in unison, praying in their own language, out loud, with George! As the people prayed, I bowed my head. When the prayer was over we handed out tracks and Bible studies for children and adults that were in their own language, Creole. The people eagerly reached for them. We ran out before everyone had a chance to receive one. I wish we had more! Geraldo helped us pass out some of the food we still had.

"Jezi Remel ou (Jesus loves you)," we told the parents. The kids were each given one piece of candy.

Then, the kids in the candy line began pushing each other. Next, the parents were trying to grab candy too. ...They were swarming like flies.

Pastor John passed out handfuls of trail mix and beaded bracelets made with the colors that were just like the shirts to remind them of the gospel presentation that they had just heard.

Then, the kids in the candy line began pushing each other. Next, the parents were trying to grab for candy too. Suddenly, little kids were trying to go under my arm for candy. They were swarming like flies. I thought of the crowds thronging around Jesus.

Craig yelled, "Get in the truck, we are done!" We still had candy, but we responded. He discretely shoved the candy under Geraldo's shirt. I told Geraldo that I would give the bag of the gospel presentation with the recording and tee shirts to Craig to give to him later. I thought that if I left it right then, in front of the crowd, he would be mobbed.

We got in the truck and took off. A lone boy chased us around the corner. He kept running after us, as fast as he could. It reminded me of the people who were so desperate for God that they followed Jesus with all of their might.

When we were way out of the sight of the crowd, Pastor John threw a big bag of trail mix to the child. The child's face beamed as he picked up his treasure and then waved back at us. This was why we came to Haiti.

Chapter Thirteen: Divine Appointments
Study It!

1. Proverbs 3:6 says, "In all your ways acknowledge Him, And He shall direct your paths." Jan says that God has set up divine appointments for you, if you should decide to take them. What does that mean?

2. Define divine appointment.

3. Why would God have divine appointments for everyone?

4. When the author met Pastor Fredrick, she felt like she was in the presence of a president or some kind of king. Have you ever met an ordinary person that you felt that way about? If so, describe the situation.

Chapter 14

R EROUTING A HURRICANE

Prayer is the key to any successful venture we do in life. It unlocks miracles, it sets people free. The power of God is unleashed to do amazing things! When our little group earnestly prayed, God changed the course of a hurricane. As you pray, God can change many things, maybe even the course of history. Don't be afraid to tell God your deepest secrets, your greatest concerns and then praise Him, and listen for his answers!

I did not feel disappointed that we had to leave Haiti. The American Airlines evacuation did not upset me even though it shortened our trip. I did not think that Hurricane Tomas would harm Port-au-Prince, we had prayed too long and hard for the people who lived here. We had ridden in their streets and walked their paths. We had eaten their food. We had a huge interest in their welfare. We had done what God had called us to do, packing His plan into the days that we had been there.

Some of our meals and lodging money was refunded by the base camp because of our shortened stay. This allowed our team to have the resources to leave money for Pastor Bellande's orphanage and for the Haitians that helped at the base camp cooking and cleaning and for Craig, our beloved guide who had quit his job to come to Haiti for the last five months.

We left Port-au-Prince on Thursday morning, and Hurricane Tomas hit Haiti on early Friday morning.

Clicking on the TV at home in the safety of our living room, we hung on to every word the news anchor was saying, intently listening to the incoming reports regarding Haiti.

> *The news reported that Haiti had dodged a bullet.*

The pictures of the rain and flooding were washing over the screen in the very streets we had recently walked. It seemed surreal that we had just been there and now here we were in the luxurious comfort of America in our own living room. Never before had I thought of my own living room as an oasis.

The news reported that Haiti had dodged a bullet. Hurricane Tomas did not have a direct hit on Port-au-Prince. It had changed is course at the last minute. The news stations were stunned.

Port-au-Prince got rain, and there was flooding, but nothing like it could have been, if it had hit directly. If Port-au-Prince had been hit directly, it would have devastated the millions of people living in tents and make shift homes. God had answered our prayers by changing the path of the hurricane!

A New Threat

The other news we heard was not as good, cholera was now spreading to Port-au-Prince. It had started in Cap Haitian a couple of weeks before. The UN had not wanted to admit it, but reports were coming out of Haiti that a UN camp from Nepal had not properly disposed of their sewage. The sewage had been allowed to seep into the Artibonite River, never before had cholera been a problem in Haiti. This strain of cholera was now getting a stronghold in the water and on the land that could last for decades. Cholera, a disease characterized by vomiting and watery diarrhea is easily preventable with clean water and proper disposal of waste. It is easily curable with a solution of salt and sugar, but in people without clean water or sanitary conditions it can spread like wildfire.

This strain of cholera was now getting a strong-hold in the water and on the land that could last for decades.

Cholera is a strange disease that can infect one

person and they have no symptoms, yet infect another person and kill them in only a couple of hours. In this country where everything is hard to get access to, the simple salt and sugar solution needed, can be almost impossible to find.

Rioting had started in Cap Haitian and was now in Port-au-Prince. The Haitian health department sent out a team of men to cover the city looking for the dead. The team roamed the streets wearing yellow moon suits; they sprayed the dead bodies they found with a chlorine disinfectant. No wonder they are rioting! The people are terrified!

Cholera is a strange disease that can infect one person and they have no symptoms, yet infect another person and kill them in only a couple of hours.

I e-mailed the base camp, and found out that cholera had not yet spread to the people of the church or the small tent camp or the base camp. I felt relieved.

Chapter Fourteen: Rerouting a Hurricane Study It!

1. Jan says, "Don't be afraid to tell God your deepest secrets, your greatest concerns, and then praise Him, and listen for His answers." Write down one of your greatest concerns. Make it a prayer.

2. Remembering answered prayers builds our faith. Write down one of your prayers that God has answered in the past.

3. Read James 5: 16-18. Jan says that you can change the course of history if you pray. Write down something or someone that you could pray for that could change the course of history, if your prayer was answered. Pray, and then dare to believe that it will be answered!

4. Compare and contrast a hurricane and prayer. How are they alike? How are they different?

Chapter 15

E PILOGUE: MAKING A DIFFERENCE

"Why are you going to Haiti, Janice?" my brother, Carl asked me on the phone one day. "Do you love those people? Because without love you might as well not go!" he said. His question echoed in my being. I pondered his question. Was I going to Haiti for the right reasons? Did I love the people of Haiti? I prayed and asked God to give me love for the people of Haiti. Love is the greatest reason for doing anything. After much thought and consideration, I decided, "Yes, I did love the people of Haiti!"

God created you to make a difference in this world with His love. Just like one drop of water at a time may someday create a huge lake if given the right environment. One act of love done by one person, strung together with acts of kindness by others, will someday make a huge difference! Here is your opportunity! Love openly, love unconditionally, love with every ounce of your being! You will never regret it. You will change the lives of the people that you encounter with God's love.

If you find your heart hollow and drained of love, He can fill it. It is God's plan that we love through Him and not in our own strength. We need only to ask. He delights in answering that prayer.

A year has passed since our trip to Haiti. God has done great things in that time frame and continues to do them!

Pastor Bellande is almost done building a new orphanage to house more children in Port-au-Prince.

The church finally received their building, which was stuck so long in customs. They have started more churches and reached more people with the gospel in many different areas of Haiti.

The shelter that our guys worked on building was later completed by a team from Oregon. They now use it to have Bible studies, to give out medicine, for medical clinics, to cut the people's hair and to do many other activities. It is a place that the church can use to touch and bless lives.

It is awesome to think that God uses each team to build upon the next teams work.

The church is making great progress in helping the people learn to become self-sufficient. It has built a bakery and is experimenting raising tilapia and chickens.

They have dug a well, where the people come to get fresh water for drinking and bathing, which is critical in the fight against Cholera. It made me think of what Paul said,

"I have planted, Apollos watered; but God gave the increase."

-1 Cr 3:6 (KJV)

As you have peered through this window, you have glanced through time at a different culture and people, a different world! What did you see?

The trip we took was short, but it was part of God's plan to touch lives at that time, in His way.

This is but a brief glimpse of Haiti in a minuscule slice of time. As you have peered through this window, you have glanced at a different culture and people, a different world! What did you see?

You have met some of the people in Haiti and heard the cry of their hearts; you have traveled their dusty streets and seen some of their looming challenges. What will you remember?

Will you answer the call of the plans for you? Your God designed adventures await you!

Will you cry out to God as an ordinary person in history, to expand your horizons? And if you do, what will you do with the secrets that God whispers to your heart in the quietness of your everyday life?

Will you answer the call of the plans that He has created for you to live? Where will you go? What will you do? You don't have to go to Haiti.

God may call you to go somewhere else. Maybe you will be sent just across the street to the new neighbor or to the next block over to help at the local elementary school.

It all begins in a simple, but life changing way. Have you invited Jesus to be your Savior? Do you believe that He died on the cross for your sins and rose from the dead on the third day? If you believe in Jesus, a connection with the living God is just a prayer away. Talk to God and tell him that you believe that Jesus, His son, died on the cross for your sins (things that we all do that are wrong). Jesus took the punishment for your sins on the cross and then became alive again. Tell God that you want to give your life to Jesus and start your new adventure, living your life for Him. The Bible says in 2 Cor. 5:7 that if you are in Christ you will become a new creature. You will get a whole new beginning, and be changed inside! Just like turning the page in a book, a whole new chapter of your life is possible.

Your God designed adventures await you! The passport to living in God's supernatural plan is yielding to your Creator everything that you are and all of your plans. It is being willing to do the plans He created especially for you to live. You will shine like the Son, with His brightness running through your veins. You can change the darkness of this world into the light of God's glory.

On which plane will you live your life? You can choose to live in the ordinary plane of your flesh, where you control your own comings and goings or you can make the hard choice, to live the supernatural life by making Jesus your life.

It is in a plane that is above the realm of this world, where God is allowed to work in you and through you and amazing things that would otherwise be impossible begin to happen. But, God will never force you.

Smith Wigglesworth said it best, "God has a plan beyond anything that we have ever known. He has a plan for every individual life, and if we have any other plan in view, we miss the grandest plan of all."

Chapter Fifteen: Epilogue: Making A Difference Study It!

1. Read 1 Corinthians 13:3. Jan says, "Love is the greatest reason for doing anything." Do you think this is true? Why or why not?

2. The author says, "God's plan is that we love through Him and not in our own strength." How is this possible?

3. In this chapter the author questioned, "As you have peered through this window, you have glanced at a different culture and people, a different world! What did you see?" Briefly describe what you saw.

4. Jan asks if you have made Jesus your Savior. If you have not done that yet, take the time right now to pray a prayer and give your heart and life to Jesus Christ. If you have trouble knowing what to say, reread the chapter for more insight.

5. Read Matthew 16:24-26. Jesus talks about living your life on a different plane than the world does, by denying yourself and following Him. How can this be accomplished in your life? How can you find your life, if you lose it? (verse 25).

6. Are you determined to answer the call of the plans that God has for you? Why, or why not? If so, what can you do to take the first step?

Notes

Chapter 1

1. Wikipedia, *2010 Haiti earthquake*, http://en.wikipedia.org/wiki/2010Haitiearthquake (as of Jan 9, 2013,20:28 GMT).

Chapter 4

1. The Jerusalem Post, *ZAKA in Haiti*, http://www.jpost.com/PromoContent/ZAKA(as of Jan 21, 2010).
2. U.S. Dept. of State, *Travel Advisory: Haiti*, http://travel.state.gov/travel/cis_pa_tw/tw/tw_46 32.html (as of June 24th, 2010)
3. Barnett, Tommy, First Assembly of Phoenix. Quote used by permission.

Chapter 14

1. NBC News, *Battling to Control Haiti's Cholera Epidemic*, http://worldblog.nbcnews.com/_news/2010/11/1 9/5495446-battling-to-control-haitis-cholera-epidemic?lite (as of Nov 1, 2010).

Chapter 15

1. Smith Wigglesworth, *Smith Wigglesworth Devotional (*New Kensington: Whitaker House,1999), p.13.

Contact Me!

I would love to hear from you! To contact me, send an e-mail to:
janhofstra8@gmail.com

To order more copies go to amazon.com or createspace.com/4234813.

Made in the USA
San Bernardino, CA
14 October 2013